Creating Campus
Community

William M. McDonald
and Associates

With foreword and afterword
by Parker J. Palmer

Creating Campus Community

In Search of Ernest Boyer's Legacy

JOSSEY-BASS
A Wiley Company
www.josseybass.com

Published by

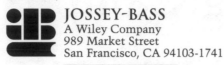

JOSSEY-BASS
A Wiley Company
989 Market Street
San Francisco, CA 94103-1741

www.josseybass.com

Jossey-Bass books and products are available through most bookstores. To contact Jossey-Bass directly, call (888) 378-2537, fax to (800) 605-2665, or visit our website at www.josseybass.com.

Substantial discounts on bulk quantities of Jossey-Bass books are available to corporations, professional associations, and other organizations. For details and discount information, contact the special sales department at Jossey-Bass.

We at Jossey-Bass strive to use the most environmentally sensitive paper stocks available to us. Our publications are printed on acid-free recycled stock whenever possible, and our paper always meets or exceeds minimum GPO and EPA requirements.

Library of Congress Cataloging-in-Publication Data

McDonald, William M., 1958-
  Creating campus community : in search of Ernest Boyer's legacy / William M. McDonald and associates.— 1st ed.
      p. cm. — (The Jossey-Bass higher and adult education series)
Includes bibliographical references and index.
  ISBN 0-7879-5700-3 (alk. paper)
  1. Boyer, Ernest L. 2. Campus life : in search of community. 3. College students—United States. 4. College environment—United States. 5. Community. 6. Universities and colleges—United States—Administration. 7. College presidents—United States—Attitudes. I. Title. II. Series.
  LA229 .C27 M33 2002
  378.1'98—dc21

2002000938

FIRST EDITION
PB Printing   10 9 8 7 6 5 4 3 2 1

Contents

Foreword   ix
Parker J. Palmer

Preface   xvii

The Boyer Center   xxv

The Contributors   xxvii

1   An Agenda of Common Caring: The Call for
Community in Higher Education   1
E. Grady Bogue

2   Creating Community in a Complex Research
University Environment   21
Betty L. Moore and Arthur W. Carter

3   Beyond Rhetoric: Composing a Common
Community Experience   45
Cynthia A. Wells

4   Modeling Community Through Campus
Leadership   69
Larry D. Roper and Susan D. Longerbeam

5   A Lab Without Walls: A Team Approach to
Creating Community   93
*Cathy Eidson Brown, J. Mark Brown,
and Robert A. Littleton*

6   Promoting Community Through Citizenship
     and Service   121
     Jean L. Bacon

7   Absent Voices: Assessing Students' Perceptions
     of Campus Community   145
     William M. McDonald

8   Conclusion: Final Reflections and Suggestions
     for Creating Campus Community   169
     William M. McDonald and Associates

Afterword: The Quest for Community in Higher
     Education   179
     Parker J. Palmer

Index   193

Foreword

Parker J. Palmer

It was . . . obvious to him . . . that there is far,
far more that unifies all of us human beings than
that separates us. Thus it was that his strongest
impulse. . . was always to make connections. He
took it as his daily task to form bridges. Bridges
between ideas. Bridges between institutions. And
most important of all, bridges between people.
  From the eulogy by Ernest Boyer Jr. at his father's funeral

One of my few regrets is that I never had a chance to get to know
Ernest Boyer Sr. especially well. I never sat with him on a committee, never worked with him on a project, never had a long and
leisurely conversation with the man. And yet, like almost everyone
else in higher education, I usually referred to him as Ernie, as if he
were an old and good friend.

In his writing and speaking, Ernie Boyer had qualities that led
his readers and listeners to regard him as a trusted companion. Obviously, he was intelligent, thoughtful, insightful, and well-read.
More important, he was a person of plain speech, moral sensibility,
spiritual openness, and practical wisdom. But, above all else, he was
a graceful man—a man full of grace.

The writers brought together for this book explore Ernie
Boyer's many contributions to the renewal of community in higher

education, and each writer, on his or her own campus, has sought to extend the Boyer legacy. They know, better than most, that cultivating community is a complex challenge in the midst of an academic culture infamous for its individualism, judgmentalism, and competitiveness. And they have much to teach us about how these obstacles can be overcome.

But before we get too entangled in those complexities, I want to name a simple truth: Ernie Boyer's contribution to the renewal of community in higher education is found not only in his thinking, his writing, his speaking, and his projects. It is also found in his personal embodiment of grace.

While Ernie Boyer was among us—with his integrity, his compassion, and his commitment—the academy felt a bit more like a community to all who knew him or knew of him. We had in him a formidable advocate for those fundamental human virtues that make community possible. He respected us and we respected him. He trusted us and we trusted him. He loved us and we loved him. Though he is no longer with us, these qualities of selfhood continue to do their work. No one who saw them embodied in Ernie Boyer can deny their possibility or their power, despite the fact that academic culture sometimes seems to scorn such elemental virtues.

The simple truth about community is that it gathers around such personal virtues shared and multiplied. That truth becomes more pointed when we turn it around: community cannot, and will not, gather around smallness of mind, tightness of heart, banality of spirit, frenzy masquerading as efficiency, myopic views of reality, faddish techno-babble, obsession with the bottom line, or the fear that is masked by arrogance in too many intellectuals' lives.

In the absence of personal grace, it matters not how many programs we create to "build community," how many trained facilitators or tested group processes or state-of-the-art workshops we budget for and buy. Every community-building project reported in this book, I wager, owes its ultimate success not to strategies and tactics but to the qualities of selfhood manifest in the leaders of those projects. Human identity and integrity are the strange at-tractors of community, and when those qualities are not available among us, you can kiss community good-bye.

It may sound like I am headed toward a pious counsel of perfec-tion here: Show me good people, like Ernie Boyer, and I will show you community. But that is not where I am going with this. I want instead to pursue a critical question: Is it possible, in higher educa-tion, to create conditions that can help all of us grow our own iden-tity and integrity, to become strange attractors of community, each in his or her own way?

In asking this question—let alone trying to answer it—I swim upstream against a widely held (although often unconscious) con-viction that while it is possible to "grow" the store of knowledge we hold and the skill with which we use it, it is not possible to grow the human soul. Or, if it is possible, "soul work" is out of place in higher education and should be left to the family, the therapist, or the religious community.

But I believe that soul work, rightly understood, is higher edu-cation's proper domain, and if we fail to make room for it, we fail to educate in any meaningful sense of the term. Indeed, I believe that all education is a process of forming or deforming the human soul—whether or not we understand, acknowledge, or embrace that fact. The only question is whether we will be thoughtful about that process and try to direct it toward the best possible ends.

My case was recently made in an unexpected place: the newslet-ter of Phi Beta Kappa, an honorary society better known as an ad-vocate of pure intellect than as a friend to the things of the soul. In the Autumn 2000 issue of *Key Reporter*, Leroy S. Rouner, professor of philosophy and religion at Boston University, wrote:

> The best thing ever written on the philosophy of educa-tion is Plato's *Protagoras*, in which one of these Athen-ian rich kids wants to study with Protagoras, a Sophist, an ethical relativist who will teach the kid how to make

a good speech without knowing what justice or whatever really means. The young man, one Hippocrates, asks Socrates to make the arrangement for him. But Socrates asks him the crucial question about education, and that is, "If you study with this fellow, what will he make of you?" This is not a question that most college deans' offices like to talk about in this *post in loco parentis* era. Still, the fact is that a college education feeds an adolescent in one end and gets a young adult out the other. In the process of those four years that person has changed significantly, and you and I have been agents of that change.

We say, "Hey, listen, I just teach history. I'm not their mother or their priest or their shrink." That's true. A college is not a family or a church or a hospital. Still, what happens, in the course of what we do, is soul making.

To prove Professor Rouner's claim, all we need to do is recall the professors who have influenced the formation of our own souls, for better or for worse. But I believe that we can and must extend his thesis beyond the relations of individual teachers to individual students and reflect on the formative, or deformative, power of academic culture itself.

That culture has been dominated by a theory of knowing that has too often deformed the souls of educated people. Sometimes called objectivism, this theory asserts that to know anything truly and well, the knower must remain at a distance from the known. According to objectivism, human subjectivity—the domain of the soul—is a vast sinkhole of shadow, bias, prejudice, ignorance, and error that must be kept apart from "the known." Whether the object of knowledge is a natural phenomenon, a period of history, some form of human behavior, or a literary text, the knower who draws too close to it runs the risk of tainting its purity with his or her subjective distortions.

This theory of knowing has been translated into a pedagogy whose main motif is "distance"—keeping teachers at a distance from their students, students at a distance from each other, and teachers and students alike at a distance from the object of their study. The result has too often been an "educated" person who has a lot of knowledge about the world but little or no sense of personal connection with the world that knowledge points to. Objectivism sets the knower apart from the known, thus setting the actor apart from the world he or she inhabits, creating what might fairly be call "educated amorality." Because the human self is inherently relational—created in, through, and for community—the distancing motif of objectivism too often leads to the deformation of the human soul.

Exactly what forces formed Ernie Boyer's soul is, to say the obvious, beyond my knowing. His character, like yours and mine, was crafted by many forces, a process ultimately shrouded in mystery. And even if I knew how to clone Ernie Boyer's nature, I would not want to do it; I love diversity too much to pursue such an Orwellian nightmare! But, knowing what I do about Ernie Boyer's biography, I dare say that his sensibilities were shaped in part by his education— an education in which distance is overcome by connectedness, in which learners are brought into relationship to, and responsibility for, the world that their knowledge is about.

One name for this kind of education is *liberal arts*. That ancient course of studies is so named, not because it is liberal in the ideological sense but because it aims at liberating us. Liberating us from what? From all external forms of tyranny, of course, and from internal tyrannies as well—especially from the aforementioned "smallness of mind, tightness of heart, banality of spirit, frenzy masquerading as efficiency, myopic views of reality, faddish technobabble, obsession with the bottom line, or the fear that is masked by arrogance in too many intellectuals' lives." Education should liberate us from the arrogance that we are either set apart from the world or perched above it all.

The aim of liberal education is to evoke from every person his or her unique version of the virtues we saw embodied in Ernie Boyer. It does so by focusing on the world, of course—the world of physical reality, of social exchange, of historical dynamics, of imagination and ideas. But we study these worlds through the lenses of the humanities and the social and physical sciences, not only to discover what is "out there" but also to discover what is "in here." Every discipline in the liberal arts, rightly understood, holds a mirror to our own condition, reflecting who we are as physical creatures, as social animals, as beings who think and feel and dream.

To separate "in here" from "out there" is to make a distinction without a difference, for the two are continually interacting to co-create what we fondly call reality. If I bring to the world an inner life riddled with arrogance, or envy, or fear, I help co-create individualism, judgmentalism, and moral indifference. But if I bring a different set of inner realities—humility, or openness, or faith, or fellow-feeling—I may help community to emerge among us. Liberal education is rooted in the time-tested Socratic dictum that "the unexamined life is not worth living." We can and should enlarge that dictum into a social principle with which I believe Socrates would agree: if you choose to live an unexamined life, you do not have the right to inflict it on other people!

When we understand the connections between inner and outer reality, and when we commit ourselves to educational soul work with the same skill and intentionality that we commit to budgets and policies and programs, we will find that it is possible to raise up more Ernie Boyers and fewer barbarians. We can start to reverse the situation that Professor Rouner describes when he writes in *Key Reporter*: "There are probably more genuinely brilliant people in American higher education today than there have ever been in the past. At the same time, there is probably less genuine human wisdom available than there was a generation or two ago" (*Key Reporter*, Autumn 2000, 66(1), p. 5).

As we examine the contributions Ernie Boyer made to the renewal of academic community through his ideas, his policy proposals, his suggestions for structures and strategies and tactics, and as
we ask how we can extend the Boyer legacy, we must remember a
simple truth: the key to community is the capacity planted deep in
the human soul to open up, to reach out, to give and take in a fabric of morally persuasive relationships. And when those qualities
are lacking in us and among us, "community" will be an artificial
and fragile facade. We must remember, too, that we have at our disposal one of the greatest vehicles for soul making and community
building known to humankind—the one called education.

I dedicate this book to my family—
Anne, Margaret, and Hannah.
Their unconditional love and abiding faith
sustain me at all times.
They are my true community.

Preface

Ernest L. Boyer Sr. served as president of The Carnegie Foundation for the Advancement of Teaching for sixteen years (1979–1995). Under his leadership, The Carnegie Foundation published numerous books and reports describing the challenges and opportunities faced by colleges and universities across the nation. Of particular interest is that Boyer valued connections and believed that colleges and universities could create a community of learning that would serve as a model for the nation (McDonald and others, 2000). Specifically, he believed that "all parts of campus life—recruitment, orientation, curriculum, teaching, residence hall living, and the rest—must relate to one another and contribute to a sense of wholeness" (Boyer, 1987, p. 8).

In 1990, The Carnegie Foundation published a special report titled *Campus Life: In Search of Community*. In this pivotal report, Boyer addresses the increasing concern for the declining state of community in higher education. His examples include the growing number of problems resulting from inappropriate student behavior and from the competing interests, ideologies, and purposes within colleges and universities. In addition, the student population is becoming increasingly transient, and academic pursuits are not the key focus of students' lives.

Having described the problems associated with a lack of community in higher education, Boyer provides a new model of community that aims to build bridges between "both academic and civic standards, and above all, to define with some precision the enduring values that undergird a community of learning" (p. 7).

To understand Boyer's model, we must first understand what he actually meant by "community." How does community translate into real-life rules and principles? Even though it's impossible to convey everything that's important about his community model here, we can illustrate some key points. Basically, Boyer felt that a college or university should be

- An educationally purposeful place where learning is the focus

- An open place where civility is affirmed

- A just place where persons are honored and diversity pursued

- A disciplined place where group obligations guide behavior

- A caring place where individuals are supported/service is encouraged

- A celebrative place where traditions are shared

To date, no follow-up report has been generated concerning how Boyer's (1990) work influenced the ongoing state of community in higher education. Specifically, did *Campus Life: In Search of Community* inspire the creation of models for building community on campus? If so, have these models been successfully implemented? If so, how can these models be replicated and generalized to other campuses that are seeking to create community among faculty, staff, and students? And finally, how have students been given a voice concerning building community on campus? *Creating Campus Community: In Search of Ernest Boyer's Legacy* has been written to answer these questions.

Boyer's Legacy

This book reviews the impact of Boyer's leadership, as well as the current state of the higher education community in a number of ways: a review of the current calling of campus community is explored; students' perceptions of community, based on varying institutional variables, are identified and described; community-building models (inspired by *Campus Life*) at five different colleges and universities are described; and new and developing community visions are identified, along with the next steps higher education must take to reclaim and strengthen community on campus.

Finally, this book is intended to be a resource for practitioners—faculty, staff, and students—who seek to cultivate and maintain the spirit of community that should undergird the collegiate experience. As its authors, we believe the combination of practical suggestions and new community models will be a valuable tool for colleges and universities interested in creating a stronger sense of community at their respective campuses.

Overview of the Contents

The uniqueness of this book will be demonstrated in the combination of authors and models that are included. Some of the authors, such as Parker Palmer, Grady Bogue, Larry Roper, and Betty Moore, are nationally known, respected authors and leaders in higher education, with significant contributions and numerous publications concerning building community at colleges and universities. Others have limited-to-little publishing experience but have created specific community-building models based on Boyer's (1990) work. The five institutions described, in combination, reveal connections among a number of institutional types: those in different geographical regions across the country, large public and small private institutions, and institutions with varying missions (research and liberal arts). Consequently, the power and utility of Boyer's (1990) model of community demonstrates a capacity for building bridges in different institutional settings within higher education.

In the Foreword, Parker Palmer reminds us that Ernest Boyer called us to affirm a new vision of community for higher education to promote the common good for society. Palmer believes that Boyer did this by being a trusted companion and through his plain speech, moral sensibility, spiritual openness, practical wisdom, and, most important, his personal embodiment of grace.

Chapter One, by Grady Bogue, explores the true calling for higher education to create community among all constituents at a college or university. This chapter explores the current state of community, that is, the variables and the stakeholders that help shape community in higher education. Concrete examples are provided in other chapters. Beginning in Chapter Two, for example, five institutional case studies illustrate how Boyer's legacy has inspired new models for community development. Chapters Two and Three provide two institutional examples—one public research university and one small, religiously affiliated college—that review institutionwide strategies for creating community. Chapters Four, Five, and Six provide three specific program initiatives for creating a sense of community. Both public and private institutional models are provided.

Chapter Two, by Arthur Carter and Betty Moore, describes the process through which the Office of Student Affairs at Penn State University used the community principles as a foundation for guiding the division's strategic planning process and implementation of its educational programming and student services.

Chapter Three, by Cynthia Wells, describes the process that Messiah College followed for rebuilding the common sense of purpose that should anchor a religiously affiliated liberal arts college.

Chapter Four, by Larry Roper and Susan Longerbeam, describes the Division of Student Affairs Campus Compact at Oregon State University.

Chapter Five, by Cathy Brown, Mark Brown, and Robby Little-ton, describes Carson-Newman College's Ernest L. Boyer Laboratory for Learning in which teams of faculty, staff, and students are charged with the responsibility of creating community through a seamless web of curricular and cocurricular educational opportunities.

Chapter Six, by Jean Bacon, describes a master's-level program in social work in which community is created through the search for knowledge, teaching, and community service.

Chapter Seven, by Bill McDonald, reviews a national study using the College and University Community Inventory (CUCI)— an instrument designed to measure community for students in colleges and universities; measurements are based on institutional variables such as regional location, size, and Carnegie classification.

Chapter Eight, by McDonald, Bacon, Brown, Brown, Carter, Littleton, Moore, Roper, and Wells, draws together the reflections and insights that have been gained from efforts to build community on the five campuses outlined in Chapters Two through Six.

The Afterword, by Parker Palmer, addresses the growing need for commitment to community in an educational environment that appears to lean more and more toward keeping people at a distance.

In conclusion, as the title of the book suggests, campus community is an evolving process. Indeed, as the book's authors, we are searching, learning, and growing as we explore the rich legacy of Ernest Boyer. In the final chapter of *Campus Life: In Search of Community*, Boyer describes his vision of a new model of community that benefits both higher education and the society by promoting the common good. This is the true essence of Boyer's legacy and a challenge that demands our best efforts to ensure that his vision and leadership are not forgotten. This book is our attempt to answer Boyer's (1990) challenge that "higher education has an important obligation . . . to define larger, more inspired goals, and in so doing serve as a model for the nation and the world (p. xiii).

Acknowledgments

I would like to express appreciation to David Brightman, editor of the Jossey-Bass Higher and Adult education series, and Gale Erlandson, past editor, both of whom encouraged me throughout the work on this manuscript. I also thank Melissa Kirk, assistant editor, for continued support as well. Their suggestions strengthened this work immensely.

I extend thanks to the Boyer Center for endorsing this book. Glen Bucher, executive director, and Don Kraybill, dean of scholarship at Messiah College, have supported this work and continue to provide the essential leadership for maintaining Ernest Boyer's vision for higher education.

I also extend thanks to Carson-Newman College and the many colleagues who have supported or participated in this project.

I am thankful for the numerous friends who have reviewed sections of the book: Tony Cawthon, Donald Kraybill, Melanie McClellan, Tim Millerick, Wynn Rosser, and Cynthia Wells. Their insights made this work more applicable for the practitioners for whom it was intended.

I am deeply indebted to my coauthors—Jean Bacon, Grady Bogue, Cathy Brown, Mark Brown, Art Carter, Robby Littleton, Susan Longerbeam, Betty Moore, Parker Palmer, Larry Roper, and Cynthia Wells—all of whom have inspired me and touched my life in ways that I will never be able to repay.

And speaking of inspiration, I was initially introduced to Ernest Boyer and Parker Palmer in my first doctoral class—the Future American College—in 1989 at the Memphis State University. Professors Todd Davis and Pat Murrell challenged fellow classmates, Ron Kovach among others, to envision what higher education could be if educators were sincere about building community among a variety of campus constituents. This book has roots in those class readings and discussions. It was my first real experience in higher education community building, and I am grateful that I had the benefit of Todd's, Pat's, and Ron's insights and wise counsel.

In closing, I am deeply indebted to Kay Boyer—Ernest's wife of forty-five years. I first met Kay when she accompanied Ernie to Carson-Newman nine years ago. I was amazed at how both of them could affirm crowds of faculty, staff, and students with personal attention characterized by quiet dignity and grace. Kay exhibited these same characteristics on two return visits to the college: for the dedication of the Ernest L. Boyer Laboratory for Learning in 1997 and in 2000 when she received an honorary doctorate for her career in health professions. The Carson-Newman faculty and staff colleagues present at the 1997 dedication will never forget Kay's gift of the Boyer name and the challenge to nurture it for future generations of students at our campus.

Jefferson City, Tennessee   William M. McDonald
October 2001

References

Boyer, E. L. (1987). *College: The undergraduate experience in America*. New York: Harper & Row.

Boyer, E. L. (1990). *Campus life: In search of community*. San Francisco: The Carnegie Foundation for the Advancement of Teaching.

McDonald, W. M., Bacon, J. L., Brown, C. E., Carter, A. W., Littleton, R. A., Moore, B. L., Roper, L. D., & Tankersley, E. (2000). *Collaboration and community: Boyer's guiding principles*. Washington, DC: National Association of Student Personnel Administrators.

The Boyer Center

The Boyer Center was founded in 1997 by Messiah College to house Ernest L. Boyer Sr.'s papers and memorabilia, his family's gift to his undergraduate alma mater. The Center's mission is to promote holistic education in school and society through programs, research, and resources that advance character, community, collaboration, and civic engagement.

The Center's first project, now virtually complete, was to catalog Boyer's papers for use in scholarship and research. Its second set of projects is no less important: to develop programs with and for students, teachers, educational institutions, and education associations and programs informed by central Boyer principles. The Boyer Center is extending commitments to community in two national projects: "Building Educational Communities: The Boyer Baccalaureate Collaborative," an extension of Boyer's *Campus Life: In Search of Community* research agenda on curricular and co-curricular programs, and a Fund for the Improvement of Post-Secondary Education (FIPSE)-funded assessment project on student affairs and academic affairs partnerships.

The Center's main program areas are:

- School renewal

- Building educational communities at the baccalaureate level

- Higher education international leadership development

- Archival research

Glen Bucher

The Contributors

William M. McDonald has been vice president for student affairs and sexual-discrimination harassment officer at Carson-Newman College since 1994. He received a B.A. from the University of North Carolina at Chapel Hill in 1980, an M.A. from Appalachian State University in 1983, and a Ed.D. from the University of Tennessee in 1996.

McDonald's professional service began in 1981. Since that time, he has acquired nine years of residence life administrative experience at Lenoir-Rhyne College, Catawba College, the University of Georgia, and Memphis State University. He joined the administration at Carson-Newman College in 1990 and served as dean for student development for four years.

McDonald is active in several professional associations. He currently serves as the codirector of a Boyer Center initiative titled "Assessing Academic and Student Affairs Partnerships for Promoting Student Learning," which is supported by the Fund for Improving Postsecondary Education. He has served as director of the Boyer Collaboratory—a consortium of colleges and universities committed to strengthening the scholarship of community, building strong educational communities, and creating and sustaining an engaged culture of learning. He has served on several professional association executive councils, including the Southern Association of College Student Affairs (SACSA), National Association of Student

Personnel Administrators, Region III (NASPA), and the South-eastern Association of Housing Officers (SEAHO). His publication and presentation interests include creating community on campus, developing model programs for faculty involvement in residence halls, assessing student perceptions of community with their college or university, blending curricular and cocurricular education on campus, conducting diversity training, making ethical decisions, un-derstanding leadership, and maintaining an effective career in stu-dent affairs.

Parker J. Palmer is a writer, teacher, and activist who works inde-pendently on issues in education, community, leadership, spiritual-ity, and social change. His work spans a wide range of institutions: colleges and universities, public schools, community organiza-tions, religious institutions, corporations, and foundations. He serves as senior associate of the American Association of Higher Educa-tion and senior adviser to the Fetzer Institute; he founded Fetzer's Teacher Formation Program for K–12 teachers.

Palmer travels widely, both domestically and abroad, conducting workshops, delivering lectures, and leading retreats. He has often been cited as a master teacher. His work has been featured by the *New York Times*, the *Chronicle of Higher Education*, *Change* magazine, *Christian Century*, CBS-TV news, and the Voice of America. The Danforth Foundation and the Lilly Endowment have supported his work with major grants. In 1993, he won the national award given by the Council of Independent Colleges for Outstanding Contribu-tions to Higher Education. In 1998, "The Leadership Project"—a national survey of ten thousand administrators and faculty—named Palmer one of the nation's "most influential senior leaders" in higher education and one of the ten key "agenda-setters" of the past decade, declaring, "He has inspired a generation of teachers and reform-ers with evocative visions of community, knowing, and spiritual wholeness."

His writing has been recognized with six honorary doctorates, two Distinguished Achievement Awards from the National Educational Press Association, an Award of Excellence from the Associated Church Press, Critic's Choice citations from *Commonweal* and *Christian Century* magazines, selection by several book clubs, and translation into several languages. His publications include ten poems, more than one hundred essays, and several widely used books, including *Let Your Life Speak*, *The Promise of Paradox*, *The Company of Strangers*, *To Know As We Are Known*, *The Active Life*, and *The Courage to Teach*.

Palmer received his B.A. degree in philosophy and sociology from Carleton College, where he was elected to Phi Beta Kappa and was awarded a Danforth Graduate Fellowship. After a year at Union Theological Seminary, he studied sociology at the University of California at Berkeley, where he received his M.A. and Ph.D. degrees with honors. He is a member of the Religious Society of Friends (Quaker) and lives in Madison, Wisconsin.

E. Grady Bogue is a professor in the Department of Education Leadership at the University of Tennessee and chancellor emeritus of Louisiana State University in Shreveport, where he served as chancellor for ten years. He received his B.S. in mathematics (1957), his M.S. in education (1965), and an Ed.D. in education administration, all from Memphis State University. From 1975 to 1980, he was associate director for the Tennessee Higher Education Commission.

Between 1964 and 1974, he held three different administrative appointments at Memphis State, the last as assistant vice president for academic affairs. He was named a distinguished alumnus of Memphis State in 1986. He served as interim chancellor of Louisiana State University and Agricultural and Mechanical College in 1989.

Bogue has written five books, and his articles have appeared in the *Harvard Business Review*, *Educational Record*, *Journal of Higher*

Education, Vital Speeches, and *Phi Delta Kappan.* He has been a consultant on planning, evaluation, quality assurance, and leadership to colleges and universities, state-level higher education agencies, and corporations. He was an American Council on Education (ACE) fellow in academic administration in 1974–75 and served as a visiting scholar with the Educational Testing Service in 1988–89. During his ACE fellowship year and the following five years with the Tennessee Higher Education Commission, he was director of the Performance Funding Project, which developed and implemented one of the first state-level performance incentive policies in American higher education. He has been a visiting lecturer in China and is an adjunct member of the faculty at Northeast University in Shenyang, China.

Jean Bacon is an assistant professor in the School of Social Welfare at the State University of New York, Stony Brook. She holds a B.A. in sociology from Warren Wilson College, a master's in social work from Adelphi University, and a Ph.D. in social work from the University of South Carolina, Columbia. Bacon has presented both nationally and internationally on the topics of university and student citizenship, collaboration in higher education, campus community, and student-centered practice and culturally competent practice.

Cathy Eidson Brown is dean for student affairs at Carson-Newman College. She earned a bachelor of general studies (1981) from Samford University and an M.Ed. in counselor education and college student personnel (1989) from Auburn University. She is currently an education administration and higher education doctoral student at the University of Tennessee, Knoxville. Before joining Carson-Newman College, Brown served for several years in various residence life positions at the Georgia Institute of Technology (Georgia Tech), Auburn University, Texas Woman's University, the University of Montevallo, and Samford University. Brown is active in SACSA and NASPA.

J. Mark Brown directs Carson-Newman's Office of News and Publications. He holds a B.A. in journalism (1986) from Samford University, an M.A. in English (1992) from the University of Montevallo, and a master's of theological studies (1997) from Beeson Divinity School. His work at Carson-Newman has included serving as a Boyer Fellow, as well as teaching courses for the departments of English, Communications, and Religion. Prior to assuming his current position, Brown was director of on-line services for Carson-Newman.

A journalist who began his career in suburban Atlanta, Brown is the former editor of The Centreville (Alabama) Press and has worked as a freelance writer and editor. His work has been published in a host of secular and religious publications.

Arthur W. Carter is assistant vice president for student affairs at Penn State University, University Park. Carter gives direct supervision to Greek Life, the Center for Ethics and Religious Affairs, the Center for Women Students, the Center for Adult Learner Services, Judicial Affairs, the LGBTA Student Resource Center, and the Paul Robeson Cultural Center.

Carter's educational background includes receiving his B.S. degree in social studies from Penn State University. He later completed his master's degree in guidance and counseling at Millersville University. Returning to Penn State, Carter received his Ed.D. in the Counseling and Educational Psychology Department at University Park in 1981. Carter is also a graduate of the 1995 Harvard University Management Development Program.

Carter is dedicated to addressing issues of student professional development, career preparation, and civic responsibility. He believes the most significant challenge facing students preparing for life after Penn State is the struggle for social justice in our local, national, and global community.

He was assistant vice president for student affairs at Tulane University from 1989 to 1991 and dean of student life at Arizona State

University from 1991 to 1998. Carter presently holds the position of affiliate assistant professor of counselor education at Penn State.

Robert A. Littleton is director of adult education at Carson-Newman College. He holds a B.S. in speech communications (1987) from East Tennessee State University, an M.S. in college student personnel (1990) from the University of Tennessee, and an Ed.D. in educational administration and policy studies (2001) from the University of Tennessee.

Before assuming his current position, Littleton served ten years in various positions within the Student Affairs Division at Carson-Newman College. Most recently, he served as director of residence life and summer programs. From 1993 to 2000, Littleton served on the administrative team of the Boyer Laboratory for Learning at Carson-Newman.

Littleton is affiliated with various professional organizations. In 1998, he participated in the Mid-Manager's Institute at Texas A&M University.

Susan D. Longerbeam is a doctoral student in the College Student Personnel Program at the University of Maryland. She has degrees from the University of California, Santa Cruz, and Antioch University. Longerbeam has held various positions in higher education, including administrator for the Department of Medicine at the University of California, San Francisco, and administrative director of the Office of Student Health Services and interim dean of students at Oregon State University. She has taught courses in college student personnel, and her presentations reflect her interest in community development and organizational change. She has engaged in community service activities such as Healthcare for the Homeless of San Francisco, Mentoring Works, and the Benton County Tobacco Free Coalition.

Betty L. Moore is the senior analyst and director for the Office of Student Affairs Research and Assessment at Penn State, where she has been employed for twenty-eight years. She has designed and implemented over ninety-two Penn State Pulse surveys (telephone and Web) on such topics as academic integrity, student drinking, post-first-year learning outcomes, civility, and campus climate, as well as the Class of 2000 Longitudinal Study, which monitors the educational impact of the Penn State Newspaper Readership project, and the 1999 Student Satisfaction Study, which was implemented at twenty Penn State campuses. She has coauthored two publications while at Penn State: *Quality of Instruction* and *Penn State As a Community of Learning,* as well as several articles and book chapters, the most recent of which is included in the 2001 Applications Manual of Lee Upcraft and John Schuh's *Assessment Practice in Student Affairs.*

Moore holds a B.S. in industrial and labor relations from Cornell University, an M.S. in student personnel and administration from Stanford University, and a D.Ed. in counselor education from Penn State.

Larry Darnell Roper has been vice provost for student affairs and professor of ethnic studies at Oregon State University since 1995. He has degrees from Heidelberg College, Bowling Green State University, and the University of Maryland. He has held numerous positions in student affairs, including director of housing, associate dean of students, coordinator of minority affairs, and vice president for student affairs and dean of students. Roper has taught courses in speech communications, ethnic studies, and community college leadership. Publications and presentations reflect his interest and experience in topics such as individual and institutional dynamics, institutional diversity efforts, leadership development, community development, and student development. He is currently serving as editor of the *NASPA Journal.* He has engaged in community service activities such as Rochester, New York's Initiative to Reduce Racial Polarization, Safe School Climate Task Force, City at Peace Project, the Peace Child Foundation, Mentoring Roundtable, Benton County Oregon United Way, and Corvallis, Oregon Chamber of Commerce.

He currently serves as the principal investigator and project director for a Kellogg Foundation grant for the Institutional Change in Higher Education Initiative (one of thirteen grants awarded nationally).

Cynthia Wells is vice provost and dean of students at Messiah College. She holds an A.B. in psychology and religious studies (1988) from Occidental College and an M.S. in student affairs in higher education (1992) from Wright State University. She is a Ph.D. candidate in higher education and student affairs at Ohio State University. Before joining Messiah College, she served for several years in various student affairs roles at Wright State University in Dayton, Ohio.

Wells is active in the American College Personnel Association. She has served as president of the Great Lakes Association of College and University Housing Officers (GLACUHO) and was honored as Outstanding New Professional by GLACUHO in 1992.

Wells' scholarly interests include faith development, narrative inquiry community in higher education, and theoretical foundations of student affairs practice. She has served as an adjunct instructor in the master's programs in higher education at Wright State University and Geneva College.

Creating Campus Community

An Agenda of Common Caring

The Call for Community in Higher Education

E. Grady Bogue

In the closing years of the twentieth century, a concern for "community" enjoyed a renewed visibility in public conversation and literature, as reflected in *Habits of the Heart* (Bellah and others, 1985) and *The Spirit of Community* (Etzioni, 1993). A similar theme entered the literature of higher education with the often-cited special report titled *Campus Life: In Search of Community* (The Carnegie Foundation for the Advancement of Teaching, 1990). The theme of "community" was also engaged in journal pieces (Kuh, 1991; Miller, 1994; Tompkins, 1992).

An important hope is carried in this opening chapter. It is the hope that those holding our colleges and universities in trust—students, faculty, staff, trustees—will understand that colleges and universities are complex, essential, and precious communities in our national life. Marketplace pressures are being increasingly felt in American higher education. We are invited to view students as customers and colleges as businesses, but there are important limitations in applying profit-sector principles in higher education. If we desire community in higher education, we need to understand the nature of the enterprise.

How are colleges distinguished from other organizations? What exactly does the term *community* signify, and why is it important to our colleges and universities? What is the nature of the community we wish to nurture in colleges and universities, and what may we, as well as our students, learn from our efforts to fashion community? What are the challenges—the impediments to the cultivation of community in higher education? These are the questions I intend to engage in this chapter.

Spaces in Our Togetherness: The Meaning of Community

Let me probe the meaning of community, especially the idea of the whole being greater than the sum of its parts, with a quick personal story. While on the administrative staff of the University of Memphis in the 1970s, I enjoyed an avocation that I found renewing: playing second French horn with the Memphis Symphony Orchestra. In the 1973–74 concert season, one of our programs concluded with Brahms's "Symphony No. 1 in C Minor." There is a lovely moment in the third movement when the second horn answers a short melodic passage carried by the first horn, and I can still remember a frisson of inner pleasure as the first horn and I exchanged melodic expressions. The closing and brisk pace of the third movement transitions into a majestic and fortissimo fourth movement.

As we moved into the symphony's finale, every member of the orchestra could sense that we were performing on a plane of musical excellence beyond our ordinary reach. The talent of the Memphis symphony would not match that of a major orchestra such as the New York, Boston, Philadelphia, or Chicago orchestras, nor perhaps other orchestras closely following, such as those in Cincinnati or Dallas. But on this evening, we were performing at a level of musical excitement that the patrons recognized, and the closing notes were followed by a ten-minute standing ovation. Members of the orchestra knew that we had enjoyed a magical moment, an emotional high, in which the combined performance of the eighty musicians clearly was something more than the sum of individual talents. There was common purpose in that moment, disciplined and responsible talent at work before and during the concert, and a common love of music. And there was a lovely experience of common pleasure that could not have flowed from solo music making.

There is a thought jewel in the fourth chapter of the Old Testament book of Ecclesiastes, which is as follows: "Two are better than one, because they have a good reward for their labor. For if they fall, the one will lift up his fellow, but woe to him that is alone when he falleth, for he hath not another to help him up. Again, if two lie together, they have heat; but how can one be warm alone?" (verses 9–11). There are works to be done, benefits to be derived, and pleasures to be enjoyed that are impossible in our oneness.

Shared purpose, shared commitment, shared relationships, shared responsibility—the need for community is a primal yearning and a practical necessity in our lives and in our society. A healthy community is one in which essential but often competing values are maintained in tensioned balance. In a healthy democracy, for example, there is a need to balance those competing ideas and impulses that are philosophic anchors for a democracy—the balance between access and excellence in education, rights and responsibility, justice and mercy, diversity and community, opportunity and disciplined effort, cooperation and competition, service and profit, self-interest and self-sacrifice, tradition and innovation.

What happens without the balance? Community degenerates. For example, cooperation taken to its negative extreme may lead us to seek the lowest common denominator of performance, in which mediocrity is not just tolerated but embraced. Competition taken to its negative extreme may lead to a dog-eat-dog mentality in which our ambition causes us to sacrifice integrity for personal profit—a moment when arrogance is ascendant. In their best expressions, however, cooperation multiplies the power of intelligence, and competition makes us stand on our performance tiptoes. It's the balancing of these and other impulses that is essential in the construction of community.

Here's another illustration of the need for balance. In *The Spirit of Community*, Etzioni (1993) notes our inclination to focus on individual rights but to neglect individual responsibilities: "To take and not to give is an amoral, self-centered predisposition that ultimately no society can tolerate. To revisit the finding that many try to evade serving on a jury, which, they claim, they have a right to be served by, is egotistical, indecent, and in the long run impractical" (p. 10).

In a word, there can be no *rights* in any community, whether societal or organizational, unless those living there also discharge their *responsibilities*. Duty is an essential but often neglected motivator in any community. It is no less so in colleges and universities, as Donald Kennedy affirms in his book *Academic Duty* (1997).

Orchestrating the tension between individual interests and community interests, between the good of self and the good of the community, is a major engagement and theme of great literature. Might we find a more potent expression of individualism than in the writings of Russian-born, America-nurtured novelist Ayn Rand? Toward the end of her novel *The Fountainhead* (1943), the multiple-page soliloquy of fictional hero and architect Howard Roark is an eloquent testimony to the power of the individual: "The mind is an attribute of the individual. There is no such thing as a collective brain. There is no such thing as a collective thought. An agreement reached by a group of men is only a compromise of an average drawn upon many individual thoughts . . . all the functions of body and spirit are private. They cannot be shared or transferred" (p. 725).

According to Miss Rand's testimony, it took her two years to compose this soliloquy, and when she consulted in the filming of the movie based on the book and starring Gary Cooper and Patricia Neal, she would not consent to the omission of a single word, though the courtroom soliloquy scene occupies some six minutes of film time, and the director of the movie wanted to reduce that scene by half.

Perhaps Ayn Rand's philosophic devotion to individualism was in some sense a reaction to the worst expressions of the collectivism she experienced while living in Russia. Neither she nor her fictional hero Roark, however, lived without relationship. And relationship is central to community.

Although the theme of community celebrates our relationships and interactions with others, it is important to acknowledge the contribution of solitude, which is certainly appropriate for a college or university. Anthony Storr has written a work titled *Solitude* (1988), advancing the idea that health and happiness flow from the ability to live in peace with oneself. The capacity to be alone, according to Storr, is as much an element of emotional maturity as our ability to cultivate relationships. The capacity to rejoice in our aloneness may thus be a mark of emotional security and maturity. Storr points to the creative achievements that writers, musicians, artists, and religious leaders have derived from their solitude.

Gibran (1973) speaks also to the contributions of solitude: "Solitude is a silent storm that breaks down all our dead branches; yet it sends our living roots deeper into the living heart of the living earth" (p. 51). However, loneliness and separation from others is one of the more difficult human experiences. Why labor to discover and create if there is no one to benefit or to share? Is the experience of beauty diminished when there is no other to join in appreciation? The human experience sings to our need for both solitude and relationship.

Although learning and creativity can take seed and flower from moments of solitude, they can also flow from our experience of community. Consider, for example, this illustration and exploration of community that is found in a true story of two thousand men and women—prisoners of the Japanese during World War II—who were forced into constructing a community in China. The story is told by Langdon Gilkey in *Shantung Compound* (1966). There were missionaries and prostitutes and a host of other diverse personalities and occupations herded into the prison compound. The prisoners were not physically abused by the Japanese but had to create community and social order without benefit of law or regulation. Such mundane but incendiary questions as who peels the potatoes for meals and how much living space is allotted for each person had to be resolved without courts or police force. They were souls without sanction, these men and women of Shantung Compound.

Aren't we more likely to share in the face of common difficulty and danger such as these men and women faced in this prison camp? Will goodness not emerge in times of crisis? Gilkey's theologically trained heart was seriously stressed to learn that the answers to these questions were not always yes. If folks in a community cared less about justice and equity than their own comfort and self-interest, what does this suggest about the patina of civilization? As did Victor Frankl in his German concentration camp experience (*Man's Search for Meaning,* 1959), Gilkey kept a diary and transformed this unwanted experience into a learning experience. He concluded that "without moral health, a community is as helpless and lost as it is without material supplies and services" (p. 76). Gilkey says, "One of the strangest lessons that our unstable life-passage teaches us is that the unwanted is often creative rather than destructive . . . this is a common mystery of life, an aspect, if you will, of common grace: out of apparent evil new creativity can arise if the meanings and possibilities latent within the new situation are grasped with courage and with faith" (p. 242).

The Shantung Compound was given to me by a friend serving as academic dean of a private college, an act of friendship and relationship. Can I be sure that my mind, in its oneness and in its solitude, would have been exposed to and enriched by Gilkey's experience and thought? Not necessarily. Our minds are immersed in great oceans of thought that flow from community. Solitude and community are thus complementary, and both are essential conditions of the human experience.

What is community? Community is a laboratory of discovery in which we come to value the possibilities found in mistake and error and serendipitous moments. Community is a venture in human learning and association, where moral meaning—concepts of justice and fairness, of human goodness and depravity, of rights and responsibility—may be factored from moments that can be both elevating and wrenching to the human spirit. Community is a dance of paradox, in which personal aspiration and personal sacrifice are found in embrace. These are lessons to be learned by faculty, staff, and students as they work to fashion community in our colleges and universities.

A sense of community in any setting signifies the presence of what I call an agenda of common caring and grace. This agenda of common caring embraces a love for soul, for standard, and for system. There is a caring for the individuals in the community, for those whose welfare is held in trust. There is a caring for a standard of excellence and integrity. And there is a caring for the policy and physical systems in which men and women relate in both work and play. Central to the essence of community is the other face of love, which is forgiveness. Readers interested in the political and practical power of forgiveness will find Bishop Desmond Tutu's book *No Future Without Forgiveness* (1999) a stimulating engagement.

In a community, there is a vision of shared purpose. There are shared values that shape and guide behavior. There is a shared giving and, yes, sacrifice to cause beyond self. Gibran (1969) urges: "But let there be spaces in your togetherness and let the winds of heavens dance between you" (p. 15). And so there are spaces in community to respect private interests and public interests. There is a space for intimacy and a space for solitude. There is a space for laughter and a space for lament, for shared moments of joy and pain. There is a space for the harmony of our togetherness and the conflict of our differences. There is a space for dark struggles and night journeys and a space for dawn arrivals of imagination and inspiration. There is a space for fellowship of conversation and a space where our silence is honored. These are also lessons to be learned by faculty, staff, and students as they construct communities of learning. But what is the special nature of collegiate community? Let us go there.

The Nature of Collegiate Community

The concept of community is central to our colleges and universities for the lessons that may be gained in the pursuit of community, some of which are cited in our previous discussion. Colleges and universities exist for purposes beyond developing knowledge and skill in our students. They are also sanctuaries of our personal and civic values, incubators of intellect *and* integrity. And so the values that mark the community of higher learning are the values that are most likely to be caught by our students.

Although his words are not specifically directed to colleges and universities, John Gardner (1990) writes:

> The community teaches. If it is healthy and coherent, the community imparts a coherent value system. If it is fragmented or sterile or degenerative, lessons are taught anyway—but not lessons that heal and strengthen. It is community and culture that hold the individual in a framework of values; when the framework disintegrates, individual value systems disintegrate [p. 113].

The unhappy fruits of such moral disintegration are loss of meaning and loss of potency. A collegiate community must be more than a collection of buildings connected only by steam lines and fiber optic cables. It must be a set of relationships that recognize and celebrate a shared vision of purpose and values.

Colleges and universities are often described as communities of scholars, communities of truth—learning communities. In one of the most familiar and informing legacies of collegiate community, Ernest Boyer (1990) characterized a college or university as

- *A purposeful community.* A purposeful community is one in which students and faculty share learning goals, and the classroom is seen as a place where community begins and where "great teachers not only transmit information, but also create the common ground of intellectual commitment. They stimulate active, not passive learning in the classroom, encourage students to be creative not conforming, and inspire them to go on learning long after college days are over" (p. 12).

- *An open community.* An open community is described as one in which freedom of expression is nurtured and civility is affirmed. The virtue of civility recognizes the dignity of every person and is built on the reciprocity principle honored in every great religious literature.

- *A just community.* Prejudice and arrogance are the enemies of a just community. Thus a just community is one that affirms diversity and "is a place where diversity is aggressively pursued" (p. 35).

- *A disciplined community.* The report describes a disciplined community as "a place where individuals accept their obligations to the group and where well-defined governance procedures guide behavior for the common good" (p. 37). Codes of conduct and security plans are attended under this community value, as are the values of courtesy and privacy.

- *A caring community.* A caring community is one where a sense of connection between student and campus is cultivated, and the nobility of service to others is emphasized. The report suggests that "students also should be brought in touch with those genuinely in need, and through field experiences, build relationships that are inter-generational, intercultural, and international, too" (p. 54).

- *A celebrative community.* A celebrative community is one in which campus heritage and traditions are central to the culture of the campus and to student life. Both the physical environment and the ceremonial traditions mark it for memory and connection in the lives of its students.

Threats to these marks of community are nicely identified by the writers, who point to disturbing realities:

> On most campuses expectations regarding the personal conduct of students are ambiguous, at best. The deep social divisions that all too often divide campuses racially and ethnically undermine the integrity of higher education. Sexism continues to restrict women. The lack of commitment to serious learning among students often saps the vitality of the undergraduate experience, and we ask: If students and faculty cannot join together in common cause, if the university cannot come together in a shared vision of its central mission, how can we hope to sustain community in the society at large? [Boyer, 1990, p. 3]

Ernest Boyer was a champion of collegiate community; as an executive of The Carnegie Foundation, he furnished a leadership impulse for the study of higher education community and the issuance of this report. He was also champion of a complementary theme. In his book *College: The Undergraduate Experience* (1987), Boyer laments the separation of competence and conscience in collegiate education, and his writings remind us that what we know is always servant to what we believe, that knowledge is servant to our values.

As we explore the essentials of campus community, this may be a moment to revisit the idea that the presence of community does not imply or require the absence of conflict. Conflict in any organization can have constructive and destructive valence. The conventional wisdom is that conflict signals individual or organizational pathology, and its presence is an alarm call to seize the nearest hose and douse the fire. This narrow view, however, misses the personal and organizational growth possibilities, the clearing-away and renewal promise that may be found in conflict. And it misses the necessity for creating conflict as an instrument to combat injustice and inequity. Leaders in any enterprise—and certainly in colleges and universities—have the responsibility to prevent unnecessary and destructive conflict, to resolve conflict that threatens the welfare and promise of either individuals or organization, and to create conflict when that instrument will serve as an instrument of growth, renewal, and justice.

Not the absence of conflict but its thoughtful orchestration is what marks the presence of campus community. Designing and nurturing a sense of community in our colleges and universities is a leadership challenge of majestic complexity. Here's why.

The Complexity of Collegiate Motive and Method

There are challenges of both motive and method to be engaged in fashioning community within our colleges and universities. On the theme of mission and motive, American higher education is expected to be both cultural curator and cultural critic, to honor heritage and to assault the limitations of common sense. This is an expectation guaranteed to keep our colleges and universities in the spotlight of public scrutiny and in the crucible of criticism.

Our colleges and universities constitute a system of both privilege and opportunity in which elitist and egalitarian impulses contend. It is a system in which the principle of autonomy, so essential in the pursuit of truth and in the nurture of democracy, is in dynamic tension with the principle of accountability, which is an antidote to professional arrogance and intellectual narrowness. Citadels of reason and persuasion, guardians of liberty and democracy, homes of discovery and dissent, engines of cultural and economic development, repositories of artistic expression, instruments of curiosity and wonder—here are mission metaphors of no small complexity and consequence.

As we noted early in this chapter, contemporary marketplace pressures on higher education constitute yet another tension in the search for the soul of American higher education, as well as a challenge to community. Will market pressures confine and distort the search for truth in the distinctive culture, and community, of American colleges and universities? There are sufficient stories in both the public and professional press in which economic interests thwart the interests of truth seeking to warrant our attention. Will college faculty become hired hands and eager entrepreneurs rather than discoverers and custodians of truth? Will college presidents become captains of enterprise rather than erudition? Will the house of intellect become a house of merchandise, where faculty are salespeople hawking their wares to students, who are credential-hungry customers? Will the college experience become one of barter and exchange between teacher and student—knowledge and credentials for time and money—rather than a shared journey of learning?

If marketplace models and ideology may prove injurious to community in our colleges and universities, so may civic models. Our nation's history in the 2000 presidential election teaches civic lessons in the power of vote and majority rule. But truth is not necessarily to be found in consensus or majority vote. The religious majority may have weighed against Galileo, but Galileo had the truth. The medical majority may have weighed against Austrian physician Semmelweiss, but Semmelweiss had the truth. The military majority may have weighed against General Billy Mitchell, but General Mitchell had the truth. The political majority in the South may have weighed against Martin Luther King Jr., but Reverend King had the truth.

Carl Sagan's *The Demon Haunted World* (1996) and Daniel Boorstin's *The Discoverers* (1983) are informing intellectual works that depict the confining effects of superstition and narrow religiosity. Colleges and universities constitute an organized assault not only on common sense but on the bondage of superstition. And so the birth of new truth may contradict conventional wisdom and discomfort majority belief. The birth of new truth is never without pain. Any sustained and reflective engagement with this idea will again mark the complexity of nurturing community in a college or university.

There are also many stakeholders who could claim a legitimate voice in addressing questions of higher education mission and purpose and in evaluating higher education performance: students, faculty, administrators, parents, civic friends and political officers, board members and alumni. Thus the often ambiguous governance processes, the concept of shared authority among this extensive range of stakeholders, and the often tedious processes of consensus decision making add to the challenge of building community.

If the complexity of mission and governance were not sufficient challenges to the nurture of collegiate community, let us consider method. Conflict and argument are integral to the work of our colleges and universities. An organization whose mission embraces the unswerving search for truth, whose methods include the adversarial testing of ideas in public forum, whose spirit embraces a certain irreverence—such an organization will not find the search for community an easy one.

If we may borrow a thought agenda from Neal Postman (1996), American educational institutions are asked to serve many gods: the god of economic utility (get a job and be a competent worker), the god of consumership (spend money and acquire material possessions), the god of technology (use tools and be efficient), and the god of multiculturalism (accent and respect differences). What you do for a living, what material things you accumulate, what toys you can use, and what your ethnicity is count for meaning. The result can be a society of hyphenated Americans—an outcome that American historian Arthur Schlesinger laments in his book *The Disuniting of America* (1992).

Postman (1996) goes on to suggest that the story of America "is a story of continuing experiment, a perpetual and fascinating question mark" (p. 71). In this view, America is a story of questions and arguments:

> Can a nation be formed, maintained, and preserved on the principle of continuous argumentation?. . . . We know what happens when argument ceases—blood happens, as in our Civil War, when we stopped arguing with one another; or in several other wars, when we stopped arguing with other people; or in a war or two when, perhaps, no argument was possible [p. 73].

As I earlier noted, then, American higher education is a guarantor of democracy and a guardian of liberty because in some ways higher education is an organized and continuous argument. Thus colleges and universities serve a critical and civilizing purpose in our society via the maintenance of argument, in serving as a forum in which contesting ideas may be evaluated in a public forum.

Continuing with our concern for method, we should observe that colleges and universities are sanctuaries for scholars seeking truth on many fronts, using diverse methods, and honoring a wide variety of philosophic assumptions about the nature of truth. Scientists want an experiment and lawyers an adversarial hearing. Mathematicians want a logical argument and theologians a search of sacred literature. Sociologists want a compilation of opinion and historians an analysis of prime sources. Novelists, musicians, and visual artists bring an interpretative spirit to the enterprise. Professional scholars look to the practical application of ideas.

Is truth revealed, discovered, or constructed? The answer may be yes to all three questions in the halls of the academy. Does truth exist independent of the observer or is the observer a part of the truth event? Again the answer may be yes on both counts. Is truth relative or absolute? Yes! Colleges and universities are companies of fact and faith—enterprises in which ideological conflict and argument are woven into their very fabric.

Here also is an enterprise often criticized for its fossilized views and processes, its reluctance and resistance to change. There is something to be said, however, for the andante majesty of higher education in its pace of change. Nurturing truth and talent is an eminently personal occupation, a work of the long term whose success is not to be found in a neat balance sheet for the current quarter or year. It is a work largely of faith and optimism.

There is yet another distraction to community in our colleges and universities. Faculty members have allegiance residing outside a particular campus, especially for research universities. They belong to various disciplinary and professional associations that can call their attention, loyalty, and caring from the campus that furnishes their financial sustenance.

To this point, I have not commented on the challenge of size as it affects our ability to form and maintain community. In recent years, I have participated in campus celebrations at three relatively small, private, religiously affiliated colleges in East Tennessee: Carson-Newman College, Lee University, and Southern Adventist University. Here are collegiate places where it is easy to feel a keen sense of community, where the size of the campus makes it possible to know almost every faculty member and student, where shared religious values furnish bonds of common commitment, and where there is a clearly articulated agenda of common caring. But what of the large university, whether public or private?

Here we depend on multiple connections to furnish a sense of belonging. A student playing in the concert band or on a varsity athletic team, living in the residence hall, participating in one or more student clubs, giving volunteer service through student organization, or holding a part-time job on campus builds his or her own network of connections that help make that student feel a part of the community of the university, whether two thousand or twenty thousand. Whether small or large, we know the practical contribution of community. Students connected to and involved with a campus are more likely to persist, to find pleasure, and to graduate.

The Soul of Collegiate Community

Is it my imagination, or is the term *soul* appearing more frequently in contemporary literature? One would not be surprised to find the word *soul* appearing in religious literature, but here is a book by Bolman and Deal titled *Leading with Soul* (1995) and one by Marsden titled *The Soul of the American University* (1994). There is an article by Frank Newman in the October 2000 issue of *Change* magazine titled "Saving Higher Education's Soul," and I have an essay titled "Searching for the Soul of American Higher Education" appearing in *100 Classic Books About Higher Education* (Fincher and others, 2001).

In 1994, I acquired two books with "soul" in their titles. One of these was a work by Thomas Moore titled *Soul Mates* (1994), and one was by Nobel Laureate Francis Crick titled *The Astonishing Hypothesis: The Scientific Search for the Soul* (1994). The themes of these two works are in rich and provoking contrast. Moore notes our inclination to see the world in terms of systems, machines, and programs— metaphors reflecting the triumph of technology. We speak of marriages and families and communities as "social systems." Mystery and essence yield to measurement and mechanics.

Moore suggests that if a concern for soul takes center place, community would be more paramount than organization and friendship more central than productivity. He further explores the importance of manners in community. This suggests that collegiate communities would be places where dignity and civility, as expressions of manners, would be celebrated. And these values are indeed affirmed as essential to collegiate community in the *Campus Life* report cited earlier. There is a spiritual center to this work. Sustaining hope and persistence in the face of dark journeys is an act of faith. And the power of faith is the centerpiece of religious thought.

Not surprisingly for a world-renowned scientist who, with James Watson, discovered the molecular structure of DNA, Crick's work centers on the scientific study of consciousness—a conceptual counterpoint to what he describes as "the hypothetical immortal soul." His "astonishing hypothesis is that 'You,' your joys and your sorrows, your memories and your ambitions, your sense of personal identity and free will, are in fact no more than the behavior of a vast assembly of nerve cells and their associated molecules" (Crick, 1994, p. 3). Such a view constitutes a counterpoint to musing about the spiritual nature of soul.

It is this idea of established disbelief that Marsden probes so well in his work *The Soul of the American University* (1994). He profiles the transformation in higher education's mission from instruction in religion, the study of moral philosophy, and a belief in God to the ascendancy of science, pragmatism, and relativism. He poses this question on science and religion: "In a world where there were no longer self evident first principles based on God-created natural laws, what happened when allegedly scientific definitions of the 'good' conflicted? How could one argue, for instance, that all humans are 'created equal' if one denied that humans were created?" (p. 375).

Now what do these ruminations on soul in general and on the soul of the university have to do with the nature of community in colleges and universities? First, scientific and religious inquiries coexist in the collegiate community. That scientific and religious inquiry can coexist—that these two wildly different assumptions about the nature of reality and the nature of human experience can both guide inquiry within the community of higher education—is a matter of some marvel.

When physicists began to talk about alternative realities and dark matter, we are led to the surprising idea that the hallway between science and religion may be shorter than we thought. When astronomers think about the "Big Bang" theory of the universe's origins, theologians are anxious to solve the scientific dilemma of an effect without a cause by reference to the Genesis scripture, "In the beginning, God created the heaven and the earth." To talk about the soul of higher education, therefore, is paradoxical, because we must acknowledge that for some colleagues the concept of soul has no meaning. And how paradoxical can it be to acknowledge that the argument over the existence or nonexistence of soul is a part of the soul or essence of collegiate community!? (The rarely employed interrobang is certainly an appropriate punctuation here.)

Writing in his thoughtful and informing *Change* article "Saving Higher Education's Soul," Frank Newman (2000) offers this note and query:

> With growing emphasis on revenue streams, introduction of for-profit activities, large-scale corporate sponsorship of research, high presidential salaries, and other trappings of the corporate world, there is new danger that the public and its political leaders will review higher education as just another interest or industry devoid of attributes that raise its interests above those of the marketplace throng. . . . It is, therefore, critical to ask what is the soul of higher education that needs to be saved? [p. 17]

Newman's article distinguishes three "soul" dimensions, as he points to the civic mission of higher education, accents the social mobility responsibility of higher education, and highlights higher education as a home for disinterested scholarship.

The Uniting Force of Curiosity and Wonder

With all this complexity in mission and motive, what provides the uniting force for the special and distinguishing character of community in American higher education? We have advanced some answers to this question. The community of higher education is a forum of fact and faith, where some truths reside in the numbers and some in the mist, but the search for truth is a uniting aspiration. It is a lively and often contentious argument over the nature of truth. It is a museum of ideas once fresh and energizing but now quaint and outmoded. It is the home of our hope, where scholars labor to solve those problems that rob men and women of their dignity, their promise, and their joy. It is conservator of the record of our nobility and our barbarism. It is the theater of our artistic impulses. It is a forum where dissent over purpose and performance may be seen as evidence that higher education is meeting its responsibility for asking what is true, what is good, and what is beautiful. It is a place where all in the community—students, faculty, staff—are called to ask what brings meaning to their lives and makes them glad to be alive. It is, above all, a community in which we celebrate the humanizing force of our curiosity and wonder, a place for dreamers of day.

References

Bellah, R. N., Madsen, R., Sullivan, W. M., Swidler, A., Tipton, S. M. (1985). *Habits of the heart*. Berkeley: University of California Press.

Bolman, L., & Deal, T. (1995). *Leading with soul*. San Francisco: Jossey-Bass.

Boorstin, D. (1983). *The discoverers*. New York: Random House.

Boyer, E. (1987). *College: The undergraduate experience*. New York: Harper-Collins, 1987.

Boyer, E. (1990). *Campus life: In search of community*. San Francisco: The Carnegie Foundation for the Advancement of Teaching.

Crick, F. (1994). *The astonishing hypothesis: The scientific search for the soul*. New York: Scribner.

Etzioni, A. (1993). *The spirit of community*. New York: Crown, 1993.

Fincher, C. (2001). *100 classic books about higher education*. Bloomington, IN: Phi Delta Kappa.

Frankl, V. (1959). *Man's search for meaning*. Boston: Beacon Press.

Gardner, J. (1990). *On leadership*. New York: Free Press.

Gibran, K. (1969). *The prophet*. New York: Knopf.

Gibran, K. (1973). *Sand and foam*. New York: Knopf.

Gilkey, L. (1966). *Shantung compound*. New York: Harper & Row.

Kennedy, D. (1997). *Academic duty*. Cambridge, MA: Harvard University Press.

Kuh, G. (1991). Snapshots of campus community. *Educational Record, 72*(1), 40–44.

Marsden, G. (1994). *The soul of the American university*. New York: Oxford University Press.

Miller, J. (1994). The continuing search for community in higher education. *Vital Speeches*, Feb. 14, 334–336.

Moore, T. (1994). *Soul mates*. New York: Harper Perennial.

Newman, F. (2000). Saving higher education's soul. *Change*, Sept.-Oct., 17–23.

Postman, N. (1996). *The end of education*. New York: Vintage Books.

Rand, A. (1943). *The fountainhead*. New York: Bobbs-Merrill.

Sagan, C. (1996). *The demon haunted world*. New York: Ballentine.

Schlesinger, A., Jr. (1992). *The disuniting of America*. New York: W. W. Norton.

Storr, A. (1988). *Solitude*. New York: Free Press.

Tompkins, J. (1992). The way we live now. *Change*, Nov.-Dec., 13–19.

Tutu, D. (1999). *No future without forgiveness*. New York: Doubleday.

2

Creating Community in a Complex Research University Environment

Betty L. Moore and Arthur W. Carter

This chapter focuses on the experiences of student services in a large, public, multicampus research setting—Pennsylvania State University. Penn State has over eighty thousand students at twenty-three campuses located throughout the state, with forty thousand at its main University Park campus. The dispersed nature of the university, the number of student services units and professional staff, the diversity of the student body, the overlapping priorities of research and teaching and student development, as well as limited resources, offer unique challenges in the attempt to build community.

Some Penn State community-building endeavors focus on the main University Park campus. Others are campuswide, including: individual campus-community alcohol partnership committees for each Penn State location, a Statement of Principle defining citizenship expectations sent out to each new student systemwide, and the Newspaper Readership Program, which provides two national and one local newspaper to every student at every undergraduate campus, in recognition of the importance of being an informed member of the community. Individual campuses have incorporated different ways of focusing on making their environments more inclusive and supportive.

Boyer's vision of integrative learning experiences for students is reflected in the fusing of student services programming with the academic mission of teaching; this is particularly difficult for large universities. New partnerships are being formed between student services staff, faculty, and members of adjacent communities. Two Boyer principles shape this emerging relationship between these partners: (1) universities are educationally purposeful communities, where faculty, students, and community members share academic goals and work together to strengthen teaching and learning; (2) universities are caring communities, where the well-being of each member is central to the learning process and where leadership is nurtured through community involvement.

In this chapter, we outline some concrete examples of how student services units within one large university are meeting the challenge of becoming meaningful contributors to the overall learning experience of students, how this vision is articulated through action plans, and how these attempts are being assessed to determine that the student outcomes achieved fit the Boyer model. It is hoped that the concepts underlying these examples can be generalized to fit other large, as well as multicampus, university settings.

Strategic Planning to Create an Institutional Culture

Establishing an institutional culture of collaboration that is shaped by the purposeful interaction of staff, faculty, and members of the larger community requires a paradigm shift—a shift reflected through strategic plans that direct the use of resources and personnel. The current strategic planning process within student services at this large university reflects a five-year planning cycle. This planning is informally designated as Penn State's Student Affairs Curriculum and constitutes the blueprint for working collaboratively to meet student needs in our learning communities.

Boyer's definition of campus life provides referents for unit directors when they are asked to specifically articulate the skills, learning experiences, and desired environment expected from the educational programming and services they offer. Boyer's principles are used as the basis of discussion and planning that crosses traditional barriers and encourages collaborative efforts to address staff planning, educational programming, grant and proposal development, and program assessment and evaluation. Linking goals and resources across service units requires deliberative efforts, especially in large university settings where offices and staff are often dispersed and overfocused on different student populations such as those living on campus, those who belong to social fraternities or sororities, or those in leadership positions.

One example is the educational programming council initiated at Penn State's University Park campus in an effort to address programming priorities on a collaborative basis. As a caring and open community, these programming efforts address issues of social responsibility and respect for others, which are critical elements for a student community with over forty thousand constituents.

Boyer's philosophy is reflected in these strategic themes for cross-unit educational programs and workshops:

- Address matters related to diversity education through coordinated efforts

- Expose students to a variety of cultures and international perspectives

- Foster a humane community in which everyone feels welcome, valued, and fairly treated

- Develop character, conscience, citizenship, respect for others, and a sense of social responsibility

- Support an expanded vision of community education to include leadership and service opportunities

As a planning tool, Boyer's concepts establish the foundation for the update of the 1997–2002 strategic plan, which calls for improved quality of basic services, educational programming, and budget management priorities that support the university mission.

Academic Alliances to Fashion a Sense of Community

Programmers focused on student issues search for consultative and instructional partnerships with faculty whose teaching and research reflect educational goals built on Boyer concepts. Faculty are asked to co-present programs aimed at influencing student attitudinal and behavioral change. Student services staff are invited to teach classes in different department settings (Psychology, Counselor Education, Leisure Studies, Sociology, Health and Wellness, Education) and to lead class discussions on classroom climate, leadership, sexual and racial harassment, personal decision making, and many other topics.

Support staff also act in partnership with academic administrators to promote active student involvement in their college education. One example of this collaboration involves establishing long-term service-learning opportunities in agencies off campus. Another example is presenting skill enhancement sessions in the first-year college courses (study skills, time management, stress management) that facilitate student learning. A third example is facilitating student participation in faculty research by offering space in the residence halls or exposure of "best practices" student fairs through in-house residence-hall TV coverage. These efforts articulate the reality of student learning that demonstrates the relationship between class concepts and real life and often takes place outside the formal classroom setting.

Faculty and staff throughout large research institutions benefit from feedback from students gained through the assessment of both in-class and out-of-class learning. Increased awareness of how today's students access and respond to information, of student preferences and need for support services, and of student personal learning styles helps make faculty and staff efforts more productive.

Place of Technology in Community Building

Today's computer technology is proving to be an important tool for helping faculty learn about resources and services that enhance the university's educational mission and that are offered by student support staff. Creation of an on-line "Resource Guide for Faculty" offers quick access for faculty who may seek material and speakers on issues like civic engagement, character development, tolerance, social responsibility, and mutual respect. This resource guide uses Boyer's principles as a blueprint. Experienced faculty are invited to access Web portals for additional information and resources related to women student issues, lesbian, gay, bisexual, and transgender student concerns, ethics and religion, career planning and decision-making approaches, academic integrity issues, and service leadership.

Faculty new to the university and those who teach large classes are provided printed materials promoting on-line resources. The resource guide assists faculty dealing with classroom issues and those who wish to increase student engagement in the larger community through involvement in academic service learning, research projects, and class projects. Student services colleagues can address classes, provide media presentations, manage groups, provide research data on student concerns, or help all parties connect with community service agencies.

Technologically enhanced on-line calendars of educational activities and events can be incorporated into instructional programs and can facilitate the development of student skills through cocurricular learning experiences.

An effort is under way to provide students with on-line access to sites for becoming involved with organizations, community volunteering, academic interest clusters, and focus groups as one way of individualizing the large campus community.

Community-building principles can be used by student services staff who advise student organizations' decisions about funding. For example, community-building questions are part of a formal guideline used by a student-managed committee for allocations—a committee that distributes approximately $1.5 million a semester that is collected through student activity fees. Groups requesting funding for projects and activities are asked to define their community-building goals and to collaborate with other student organizations to maximize the attainment of these goals. The guidelines mandated by the student boards ensure that funding decisions are responsive to issues of diversity, openness to gender, sexual orientation, and spiritual and ethical concerns, as well as sound fiscal management. The careful administration of student fees supports a myriad of student community-building activities with a minimum of dissent.

Campus Dialogues to Form a Just and Caring Ethos

Today's college students are targets for harassment and agitation from hate groups across the nation. The effort to create a hate-free environment in which differences in ethnicity, sexual orientation, and political-social perspectives are respected attests to Boyer's repudiation of hate and to the recognition that hate and divisiveness threaten the very concept of student learning communities.

Faculty in sociology and student services staff in the centers for Community Education, Counseling and Psychological Services, Residence Life, Student Health Services, as well as in the AT&T Center for Service Leadership and the College of Education, have worked together to address "hateful acts." The sense of community is thus increased by promoting the building of student coalitions, bringing nationally known speakers and media materials to campus, and enhancing intergroup dialogues.

The concept of a "just community" as one that is open and equitable to all remains somewhat elusive, even in the new millennium on our nation's campuses. Recently, students in several large research institutions have been the targets of hate messages about ethnic and sexual minorities, women, and religious groups; these hate messages act to destroy the fabric of a civil community. Campus dialogues focused on race exemplify an effort to guide discussion, to build new perceptions of those who are "different," and to bring students who have been traditionally at the margins of community into the center of a caring and concerned environment.

As a Boyer community, we also use nationally known resources for countering hate messages that target campus communities. The *New York Times* presentation, "Race In America," and the video presentation, "Journey to a Hate-Free Millennium" (which addresses hate based on sexual difference and race), in coordination with a series of faculty- and student-led discussions, strengthen community.

Community Alliance to Influence Responsible Behaviors

The Boyer principles of community have provided an effective paradigm for helping student services staff at twenty Penn State campuses initiate a major statewide effort to address students' abusive drinking behaviors. Penn State campuses across the Commonwealth of Pennsylvania have reached out to community residents, municipal officials, entertainment and hospitality businesspersons, and others to work collaboratively in addressing the outcomes of excessive alcohol consumption. For many individuals, working across town-gown barriers requires a new definition of the traditional college-community relationship, especially when dealing with a difficult topic that has implications for business, personal behavior, and community regulations. This endeavor has also involved discussions about how the institution relates to both on-campus and off-campus student residents and revisited the issue of in loco parentis.

Community leaders have recently been included in the annual convocation for incoming students to discuss and model joint expectations of the behavior and civic responsibility that is expected of members new to the area. The process of involving community leaders in traditional campus-based activities often results in a better understanding of the new generation of students, as well as in-creased opportunities for community and service learning. As of Fall 2001, all new students systemwide received a Statement of Princi-ples outlining expectations of citizens of the university community.

Community Service to Develop Leadership

Boyer's principles have served as the structure for several Penn State grant proposals to the National Center for Service Learning and to The Campus Compact. These grants emphasized the concepts of the "servant leader" and an "ethic of service" as integral to leader-ship development.

Penn State envisions student leadership as a learning outcome that grows from a combination of formal instruction and service to others. It is part of a purposeful learning community in which fra-ternity and sorority life, competitive sports, forensics, service days in community action work, and student organizational involvement all serve as leadership opportunities. The Office of Student Affairs has maintained formal, collaborative efforts to promote student leadership development in the specific colleges of Engineering, Ed-ucation, and Agricultural Sciences. Programming and instruction with these academic units reflect awareness that students need an array of skills, values, and experiences if they are to be competitive in global work environments and in constantly changing employ-ment settings. Ability to interact with others from diverse back-grounds and trained willingness to be an engaged member of a group are skills valued in today's new work settings.

Research universities have been somewhat slower than liberal arts colleagues in helping faculty integrate concepts of ethical be-havior, personal integrity, character development, and an appreci-ation of diversity as components of leadership into a curricular perspective. Teaching leadership skills is an important element of civic responsibility and can occur through experiences in student organizations, boardrooms, military situations, and classroom settings. Repeated exposure through course work, community work, activity management, student research, interaction with senior university administrators, and management of campus and systemwide elected student leadership posts creates community leadership skills.

Students new to large universities located in isolated settings face special challenges. Fresh Start is one example of a program offering community service activities for new students as soon as they arrive on campus. Fresh Start encourages first-year students to select a venue in the local community where service is valued and to complete their projects before the semester begins. Orientation for Fresh Start experience stresses the institution's expectation that first-year students be part of a purposeful, caring, and engaged community and is a viable alternative to the "party-hard" mentality often embraced by new students their very first days on campus.

Student services staff schedule additional urban experiences throughout the academic year in cities such as Philadelphia, Pittsburgh, Erie, and Harrisburg. These opportunities for community service are alternatives to traditional semester-break activities; students can volunteer to work with Habitat for Humanity, community nutrition projects, projects connected to ongoing course work, and community service that is designed to promote civic responsibility through initiatives to encourage voting and social action. Students returning to Penn State from service activities across the state and across the nation voice a commitment to addressing social, political, and economic concerns of many citizens.

Establishing Community-Building Goals for Student Services

The commitment to Boyer's concepts and the need to encourage the development of a civil and engaged community are seen as essential by all units within the Division of Student Affairs at Penn State. This is evidenced by the directors who include a summary of community-building goals, endeavors, and activities as part of their annual reports and who regularly review the specific community-building activities of individual staff within their units.

One example of student services goal setting that reflects Boyer's concept of community is Residence Life, which adheres to the principle that their role is to provide a safe, secure, comfortable, nurturing, on-campus environment that is conducive to residents' academic pursuits and personal growth while fostering a sense of community, civic responsibility, and appreciation of diversity.

The joint commitment to quality and to community building is evidenced by their staff being willing to assess, evaluate, and review the steps that have been initiated to implement their goals. By accepting feedback from students that suggests the need to further refine unit goals and convert these into action plans, Residence Life clarifies its dedication to being a cornerstone of the university's effort to structure the student environment, develop a sense of community, and nurture skills needed to act as responsible citizens by regularly discussing and establishing activities that include community-building elements—activities such as these:

- Using an educationally oriented discipline system within the residence halls

- Disseminating information about rights and responsibilities, policies and rules, and community standards

- Educating students to accept responsibility for their actions and become considerate community members

- Providing social events where no alcohol is served

- Sponsoring activities that support local social service agencies

- Encouraging and facilitating student involvement in community settings

- Providing housing arrangements such as interest and honors houses that complement educational programs

- Teaching students to become advocates for community change
- Engaging in teachable moments with students when opportunities arise
- Challenging students to learn about diversity and about how to deal with differences

Residence Life assesses the effectiveness of their community-building efforts through an annual Quality of Life survey, periodic group discussions, and special surveys on learning outcomes associated with specific programming.

Assessing Community-Building Outcomes

Measuring the quality of experience is an important dimension of reviewing the effectiveness and the value of programs and services initiated to affect the student community. Assessment demonstrates student needs, satisfaction with resources and programs, and areas for improvement in meeting the goals and visions of those focusing on creating a civil and productive community environment.

Assessment answers questions such as these:

- Is there a way to define and to measure the philosophical concepts of civility and community?
- Can we determine which factors contribute and which factors hinder the effort to build community?
- How effective are our programs and services in contributing to the goals we feel are central to our units?
- Do our programs and services result in the student learning outcomes we expect?
- Are the efforts to build a civil community equally successful across all the student subgroups within the community?

- Do the assessment results demonstrate that student services values are being communicated effectively to students?

- Are we achieving what we had hoped to achieve?

Assessment of the quality of student experiences within the context of the Boyer principles can help in making decisions about the immediate use of staff and resources or determining the format for future strategic planning. Assessment necessitates the articulation of specific and unambiguous questions and response options that help define the student services philosophy of commitment to community. Assessment also provides a language that resonates with others at large research universities and helps clarify the ways in which student services contribute to the academic mission of the university.

Assessing Purposeful Learning

The importance of the instructional function constitutes the central core of college mission statements. Willits, Janota, Moore, and Enerson (1995) examined student and faculty perceptions of the elements of what constitutes quality teaching—the foundation of Boyer's learning environment in a study titled "Quality of Instruction." A random sample of students and instructors were asked twenty-five questions related to eight dimensions of quality instruction. Students and teachers were remarkably similar in endorsing each as very important for high-quality classroom environments (see Table 2.1).

Students and instructors did differ in their evaluations that focused on providing intellectual stimulation, demonstrating the importance of the material, being well prepared, being easy to talk to, and providing feedback on exams. However, it is noteworthy how much alike students and instructors were in defining quality classroom behaviors. This study shows that students may be more sophisticated about good teaching than they are usually given credit

Table 2.1. Components of a Quality Educational Environment

Quality Instructional Behaviors	Instructors	Students
Explains material clearly	96.2%	96.8%
Makes subject matter understandable	95.9%	95.8%
Presents difficult ideas with clarity	94.8%	94.8%
Demonstrates knowledge of subject	94.5%	94.6%
Evaluates student work fairly	91.6%	93.7%
Is well prepared	97.5%	91.7%
Is enthusiastic about teaching	91.1%	89.5%
Stimulates students to think	97.8%	89.1%
Grades based on student understanding of material	84.8%	87.8%
Presentation is well organized	90.6%	87.1%
Feedback on student work is valuable	83.2%	86.6%
Is impartial in assigning grades	90.6%	86.4%
Makes material interesting	81.9%	85.1%
Clearly defines student responsibility	84.8%	85.1%
Maintains classroom conducive to learning	92.7%	83.6%
Uses class time wisely	85.3%	83.2%
Course content is well developed	87.2%	81.8%
Is easy to talk to	73.1%	81.4%
Is interested in subject matter	83.9%	81.1%
Seems to enjoy teaching	82.2%	79.1%
Is accessible outside of class	74.2%	77.5%
Demonstrates importance of subject matter	82.5%	76.0%
Stimulates intellectual curiosity	92.0%	75.4%
Provides various points of view	72.6%	72.4%
Has a genuine interest in students	72.4%	71.8%

Source: Willits, Moore, and Enerson, 1995, p. 8.

for and that their feedback on the learning environment should be respected.

Student services staff present many community-building workshops as a means of disseminating information and initiating educational discussions in out-of-class situations. An evaluation form used across units provides student feedback about learning outcomes. In addition to processing these evaluations, staff presenters are asked to indicate to what degree each of their programs fit the six Boyer principles (see Table 2.2). This evaluation process and Boyer summary can be used to verify progress toward unit goals and to assist staff in planning purposeful workshops.

Another example of including questions on community building and learning outcomes when assessing unit efforts is a recent survey titled "Impact of Sharing a Room." Students reported that sharing a room helped them

Table 2.2. Fit with Boyer Principles, Fall 2000 Presentations

Program Fit with Boyer Principle	No Fit	Some Fit	Significant Fit
An educationally purposeful place where learning is the focus	5%	12%	83%
An open place where civility is affirmed	11%	57%	32%
A just place where persons are honored and diversity pursued	15%	53%	32%
A disciplined place where group obligations guide behavior	32%	40%	28%
A caring place where individuals are supported/service is encouraged	10%	50%	40%
A celebrative place where traditions are shared	34%	55%	11%

Note: N = 157.
Source: Penn State Student Affairs Program Evaluation, Fall 2000.

- Learn about different cultures and lifestyles

- Learn how to work out problems and negotiate

- Learn how to assert themselves

- Learn how to explain ideas

- Learn how to listen to others

- Learn about classes and majors

- Learn effective study skills

- Feel more connected to the college community

- Value respect and consideration

- Recognize the needs of others

These results and those of other surveys noted in this chapter that are from Penn State's Office of Student Affairs Research and Assessment can be found on-line at http://www.sa.psu.edu/sara.

Clarification of the learning outcomes associated with sharing a room bolsters the requirement for first-year students to live on campus. Many colleges have established special residential learning communities and have made exceptional efforts to facilitate faculty-student interactions outside of class settings. Assessment helps determine the impact of these efforts and provides a baseline for further discussion.

This is especially useful when student feedback does *not* confirm the results anticipated by well-meaning staff. Lack of success can be used to redefine and redirect the next steps. Handled well, the lack of success can be motivating.

Residence Life staff were disappointed that special programming in one campus living area did not result in significant differences in the responses of those students compared to responses from students in the other living areas. The findings in a survey titled "Residence and Student Learning" indicated that first-year students in *all* the residence areas reported similar progress since their arrival in: learning how to make decisions, acquiring productive study skills, becoming involved in campus life, and meeting others from backgrounds different from their own. The willingness of the Residence Life staff to accept disappointing results and use them to help redefine their action plans for the next year suggests a genuine concern for community building.

Learning Outcomes

Assessment clarifies the role of student services in complementing the educationally purposeful climate for the college campus.

Faculty at many colleges have recently begun to emphasize the use of team projects as a means of providing students with "active learning" experiences that develop characteristics valued by the corporate and business world. A comprehensive study titled "Student Experience and Satisfaction" found that a majority of students indicate that involvement in student activities contributed to the development of their leadership abilities, communication skills, self-reliance skills, decision-making skills, ability to execute plans, and ability to work on team projects.

Relating classroom learning to real life reflects one important element of Boyer's "purposeful community" dimension. Several years ago, Penn State introduced a Residence Hall Newspaper Readership Program, which has since been expanded to both on- and off-campus students at twenty of its locations across the state. The program offers the *New York Times, USA Today,* the local community newspaper, and the campus student newspaper Monday through Friday. Student feedback has been used to refine the choice of newspapers and distribution locations, as well as to determine the relationship of the program to general learning goals considered important by the community of scholars. Results from the initial efforts were used both to justify a modest ($5 per semester) tuition adjustment and to engender the attention of faculty. Students reported that reading the newspaper regularly contributed to the quality of their overall education and had a positive impact on

- Understanding ethical dilemmas

- Discussing current issues in class

- Connecting real-life and classroom concepts

- Evaluating the use of language, arguments, and statistics

- Understanding politics and the law

- Gaining historical insight

- Developing strategies to pursue their own goals

- Being informed about national, college, and community issues

Assessing Personal Values

Personal values are difficult to impose but have considerable impact on the campus climate. For example, many campuses are experiencing problems with student drinking decisions, despite earnest efforts to regulate, educate, and offer alternative activities. Penn State has been monitoring some student drinking data for seven years, as well as the impact on campus social norms of a popular alternative activity known as "Late Night Penn State." It is clear that students think others drink more and over a longer period of time when they socialize than they do themselves. It is also clear that students tolerate social behaviors that most staff and faculty do not see as contributing to a productive learning environment.

However, these surveys do establish that there is a critical mass of peers who do not drink or who drink in a responsible manner.

They also contradict social stereotypes such as "students who don't drink don't fit in" or "students who attend alternative social programs simply drink more before or after the activities."

Modeling the values campuses feel are important may be more effective than focusing only on the dissemination of information on regulations and consequences. Assessment provides a way to allow students to represent peer values and responsible behavior.

That is not to say that information dissemination is not important. Communication about the positive characteristics of student behavior can influence attitudes and future behaviors. Assessment information from surveys on community volunteering, voter registration, and learning outcomes associated with involvement in out-of-class activities can shape positive community perspectives.

A recent survey titled "Citizenship and Voting in an Election Year" found that (contrary to expectations) 80 percent of a random sample of undergraduates over age eighteen had registered to vote and that 70 percent of those had voted in the latest election. Most students had registered in their home precincts and voted at off-campus locations. Using data on numbers of students who had voted at campus precincts did not truly reflect how many were fulfilling an important civic responsibility.

Assessment feedback often substantiates the educational purposefulness of some student experiences. One example is the relationship between the community volunteering and learning outcomes reported. Over half of the undergraduates who responded to the survey, "Community Volunteering and Service Learning," reported that they had volunteered for community service activities since coming to college. Feedback from these students suggests that community volunteering leads to understanding real-life issues, to the breaking down of social stereotypes, to seeing the need for long-term social change, and to a better understanding of people from backgrounds that differ from their own.

In addition, students felt that these experiences improved their communication skills and their understanding of their own strengths and skills. More extensive service-learning projects contributed to: achieving class academic objectives, being motivated to learn, knowing more about the world beyond campus, and feeling some control over their own education.

Students stated that their volunteer and service-learning participation improved their sense of responsibility and awareness of ethical dilemmas. They also felt more connected to the community and more aware of civic responsibilities.

Assessing Climate

Many colleges allude to the importance of a civil campus climate in their goal statements. It is difficult, however, to find out how they are evaluating their progress—for several reasons. One is that this is very difficult to do; another is that the assessment of community experiences is viewed through the perception of members of the community and is difficult to summarize; a third is that perception assessment is often challenged as imperfect research; and a fourth is that colleges may learn through their assessment measures that they have been less successful than expected or need to address discomforting questions.

Students and faculty were invited to share their perceptions of the University Park campus as a community of learning (Willits, Janota, Moore, and Enerson, 1995). Respondents were asked how well their experiences fit each of the six Boyer principles. In general, students were more positive than faculty. For both groups, those who were new to the setting (first-year students or assistant professors) were more positive than those who had been members of the community for a longer period of time.

Three telephone surveys were implemented to focus on the perceptions of undergraduate students. A random sample of students were asked general questions based on the six Boyer principles and specific questions about their individual experiences as members of the campus community (see Table 2.3).

Table 2.3. Undergraduate Students Who Felt
Their Campus Climate "Fit" the Boyer Principles

Six Boyer Principles	2001 (n = 754)	1998 (n = 640)	1995 (n = 362)
Purposeful	70%	63%	57%
Open	64%	70%	53%
Just	54%	57%	49%
Disciplined	50%	42%	46%
Caring	65%	59%	54%
Celebrative	84%	87%	70%

Source: Students Affairs Research and Assessment Penn State Pulse surveys.
(http://www.sa.psu.edu/sara/learning.shtml)

A major effort to assess climate in 1999 was the "Student Experience and Satisfaction Survey," which involved twenty Penn State campuses across the state. Students were asked to evaluate the quality of their campus efforts to create a "sense of belonging," efforts to provide a feeling of "safety and security," and satisfaction with their decision to come to Penn State.

This campuswide endeavor was difficult. It required collaborating extensively, developing generic language appropriate to multiple campus settings, and providing useful summaries so that staff, faculty, and students at any one location could more productively discuss the findings. For example, in addition to overall results, data were provided for each individual campus, for the group of campuses that had residence halls, for adult learners, and for women students. Plans are under way to design a follow-up survey, "Satisfaction Survey for Spring 2002."

Boyer emphasizes the importance of providing supportive and inclusive environments where all members of the community feel they belong. Findings from several "civility surveys" indicate that some of the results varied according to student gender, class status, and student ethnicity. These differences were further explored through the "Diversity Climate Survey" and the "Campus Climate for Lesbian, Gay, Bisexual, Transgender (LGBT) Students Survey."

The diversity study included students from the University Park campus, as well as five of the smaller locations located elsewhere throughout the state. Students were asked to identify their ethnic status as "minority" or "nonminority." An equal proportion of minority and nonminority students reported that their campus climate affected their feeling of being connected to the university, making friends, becoming involved in activities, handling academics, and having a sense of self-confidence.

Minority students at the smaller campuses did not differ from their nonminority peers in the assessment of their campus climate. However, minority students at the larger University Park campus were less likely to feel that the campus climate was supportive, educationally purposeful, just, and celebrative.

One-third of the randomly selected respondents to "Campus Climate for LGBT Students" thought that the campus climate was generally supportive of LGBT students; two-thirds felt that they personally were supportive. At the same time, many students reported hearing or seeing derogatory comments, jokes, or verbal harassment related to LGBT issues. Students may not realize the detrimental impact of such hostile behaviors.

Assessing Differential Impact

It is important when assessing campus climate, environment issues of importance to students, or the effectiveness of staff programming efforts to consider student characteristics that may affect their experiences and perceptions. The results of these surveys are more effective if they can be analyzed overall, as well as by subsamples of respondents. The demographics of importance are best determined by the specific campus population, as well as the survey topic. For example, civility issues on campus may be perceived differently by minority and nonminority students and yet differently by Hispanic Americans or Asian Americans on that campus. The effectiveness of regulations and disciplinary functions may be viewed differently by adult learners or traditionally aged first-year students. Safety and security issues may affect women and men differently.

Demographics that might be considered include: residence (on- or off-campus living arrangements), extent of involvement in out-of-class activities and organizations, subject major, work history, participation in special programs such as mentoring first-year students or academic honors classes, academic status (nondegree versus degree-seeking students, freshmen and sophomores versus juniors and seniors, transfer students, graduate or undergraduate degree-seeking students), and those who do or do not receive financial aid.

Conclusion

Creating community in a multicampus environment is a challenge. The Boyer principles help define viable guideposts in this endeavor. These concepts provide a common language and basis for collaborative discussion and planning, as well as a means for evaluating efforts to contribute to the learning experiences of students.

Student Affairs staff at Penn State structure many of their programming efforts around the value of a civil learning environment that respects the contribution of classroom, out-of-class, and community experiences. Staff articulate purposeful action plans, using the Boyer model, and assess their progress by reviewing student feedback.

Feedback from students is essential in determining whether the mission and goals of the college have been effectively communicated to students. Often these goals involve periodic and extensive discussions on the part of the entire college community. However, the rapid turnover of student generations requires continued efforts to ensure that current students understand the principles and values that underlie faculty, staff, and administrator decisions and see the relationship between these values and their efforts to create a productive learning community environment.

Best Practices

- Staff discussion among all levels of a unit is necessary to develop a common vision based on the value of a civil campus environment, focused strategic plans directing resources, and clear action steps.

- Active collaboration among students, staff, and faculty articulates learning opportunities that connect classroom instruction, out-of-class experiences, and community service.

- The Boyer model is helpful when attempting to assess such concepts as learning beyond class content, student satisfaction, civility, and community.

References

"Campus Climate for LGBT Students." (September 2000).
    http://www.sa.psu.edu/sara/pulse/74-LGBTStudents.pdf
"Citizenship and Voting in an Election Year." (November 2000).
    http://www.sa.psu.edu/sara/pulse/78-Voting.pdf
"Community Volunteering and Service Learning." (October 1999).
    http://www.sa.psu.edu/sara/pulse/volunteering_63.shtml
"Diversity Climate." (April 1998). http://www.sa.psu.edu/sara/pulse/dc98.shtml
"Residence and Student Learning." (March 2000).
    http://www.sa.psu.edu/sara/pulse/residence_life_70.shtml.
"Student Experience and Satisfaction Survey Results." (1999).
    http://www.sa.psu.edu/sara/satisfaction/default.shtml
Willits, F., Janota, J., Moore, B., & Enerson, D. (1995). *Penn State as a community of learning*. Philadelphia: Pennsylvania State University.
Willits, F., Moore, B., & Enerson, D. (1995). *Quality of instruction*. Philadelphia: Pennsylvania State University.

Note: Summary results of studies identified alphabetically and chronologically, as well as survey questions, frequencies, and significant differences, are available on request at blm1@psu.edu.

3

Beyond Rhetoric

Composing a Common Community Experience

Cynthia A. Wells

The ideal of community was central in the founding of Messiah College. The college's history is filled with images of belonging and shared identity. College spirit is evident in the friendships, athletic contests, celebrations, and rituals of transition that fill the story of Messiah College and its people. Shared meals at the dining commons provide opportunities for building relationships that sustain community. Personal sacrifice on behalf of the institution notes the legacy of individuals to the value of the college. Shared participation in a community of scholars and learners with a commitment to the practice of faith in the world undergirds affiliation with the college. The images of community have been present throughout the college's history. However, these images have not always reflected a common experience of community for the institution throughout the years.

Messiah College has been a dynamic institution since its founding in 1909. The founders shared a vision for preparing people of faith for service in the world (Sider, 1984). This core purpose has remained central. A strong focus on the theological emphases of the

The author expresses sincere appreciation to Messiah College and its former and current members who developed the ideas, programs, and practices described throughout this chapter. Special thanks to Kim Phipps and Rodney Sawatsky for inspiring both the content and completion of the chapter. The author is sincerely grateful to Donald Kraybill for his careful editorial assistance.

founding denomination, the Brethren in Christ, alongside an openness to other denominations, has also remained constant. As size, scope, organization—even the name of the college—has changed substantially over the years, the institution has struggled to readjust the notion of community to its contemporary environment. Changing demographics, increasing enrollment, and growing specialization have raised a host of issues about the meaning of community on campus.

In many ways Messiah College has not changed. The college has retained its core purpose. It has remained predominantly residential and fully undergraduate; the student body is made up of mostly traditional-aged college students. The college has not entered the arena of distance learning. All academic programs are delivered through personal interaction with faculty. Shared living and learning spaces have provided a cornerstone for building campus community; students and employees share a common Christian faith commitment.

Although these characteristics offer some promising avenues toward community, they are insufficient for composing an ongoing experience of campus community. These characteristics have functioned as baselines for the institutional understanding of community but have proved meager in times of dynamic change.

Community has been embedded in the greatest aspirations for Messiah College, its founders, its leaders, and its constituency. For scholars and practitioners interested in building community, Messiah College offers a story in which images and activities associated with community are present but insufficient. This chapter presents the narrative of an institution reclaiming its commitment to and ownership of educational community.

About Messiah College

Messiah College is a residential institution serving 2,900 undergraduate students; 90 percent live in college residence halls, campus apartments, and special interest houses. The college offers over fifty academic majors, as well as extensive study abroad opportunities and a college honors program. Messiah College is located in Grantham, Pennsylvania, twelve miles south of the state capital, Harrisburg.

Founded in 1909 by the Brethren in Christ denomination, the college was named Messiah Bible School and Missionary Training Home. Soon it was renamed Messiah Bible College, which coincided with the establishment of a junior college. In 1951, the college was renamed again—Messiah College.

In 1972, the college transitioned from having legal ties with the founding denomination to entering into a covenant relationship. Messiah College is the only institution of higher education associated with the denomination. Connections are strong through interpersonal relationships, as well as governance-dictated representation on the board of trustees. Messiah College is a member of the Council of Christian Colleges and Universities, representing a shared commitment to Christian higher education and to the shared commitment of Christian faith for educators, administrators, and students.

However, the ethos of the college is ecumenical; its faculty and students come from dozens of different traditions. Only 5 percent of the student body in 2001 is drawn from the Brethren in Christ denomination, whereas 62 percent were Brethren in Christ in 1963. The life of faith and related expectations for service associated with the theology of Brethren in Christ, however, are interwoven throughout the college experience. The challenge has been to maintain this commitment as declining percentages of educators and students enter the institution with shared understanding of this heritage. If the distinct theology of the institution was to remain vital in teaching and learning, new means of ensuring understanding of this distinctiveness and related commitments were necessary.

The college's faith commitments underline a strong commitment to and expectation for campus community. The theological heritage of the college underscores the importance of community. Communal discernment has historically been significant to the Brethren in Christ, and community remains one of ten core values of the denomination (Brensinger, 2000). Shared faith commitment is a gift to community building. Our theological diversity provides a challenge to building community. The rhetoric of community is prominent throughout the college's literature. The college affirms in its confession of faith that "God calls us to unite in the Church as a visible community of believers which celebrates God's grace in its worship and bears witness to the truth of the Gospel through its being, doing, and speaking" (*About Messiah*, p. 11).

"Significance of community" is one of five foundational values that undergird the educational mission of the institution. The description of this value expresses the Christian foundations for community of the college. In community, we "voluntarily share our lives with each other, we care for each other, we rejoice and suffer together, we worship together, and we offer counsel to one another" (*About Messiah*, p. 14). Although community is central in college literature, rhetoric has not always resembled reality. A shared experience of community has been challenged in times of transition and change.

Messiah College has experienced rapid growth that has stretched our former understanding of community. Current enrollment exceeds 2,900 students, representing a two-fold increase since 1981. Numbers of faculty doubled as well from 76 in 1981 to 150 in 2001. This rapid growth disturbed the former, shared understanding of community that depended on small campus size. With each new class now exceeding 700 students, it is impossible for everyone to know everyone else on campus.

Enrollment growth has not been the only major shift. The college offers a broader range of academic programs now than it did in the early 1970s. More educational programs in applied disciplines complement the former, predominantly liberal arts curriculum. Today over half of Messiah's students are enrolled in applied programs. Community based on common academic disciplines and personal acquaintance is no longer feasible; the parameters for building community have had to shift.

Prevalent expressions of loss in the sense of community on campus demanded new efforts to rebuild and restructure that community. The critical foundations for community-building efforts at Messiah College center on using the lens of community to clarify the rhetoric, program, and practice of existing community-building efforts. Shared purpose, identity, and common experiences support a deepened experience of community.

Four frames represent arenas in which the college has worked toward building community: (1) institutional mission and identity, (2) ethos education, (3) partnership, and (4) celebration.

Building Community Through Clarifying Institutional Identity

The principle of educational purposefulness is foundational to campus community (Boyer, 1990). The central function of a college is for teachers and learners to join in a common intellectual journey. Faculty and students must take the educational mission of the institution seriously in order for the discourse about strengthening community to be meaningful (Palmer, 1999). The importance of a distinctive educational mission is foundational to building community; this is evident in Messiah's institutional narrative.

Mission and Identity

Presidential transition provides a time to refocus the overarching purpose and vision of an institution. This was the case in the early 1990s when the Messiah College board of trustees, anticipating a change in presidents, refocused the questions of institutional identity and mission. It was critical to the board to both be faithful to the college's theological heritage and to incorporate the growth of new educational programs.

Following the 1994 appointment of the college's sixth president, Rodney J. Sawatsky, a broad representation of the college constituency revised and clarified the college's mission and purpose with the following identity statement: "Messiah College is a Christian college of the liberal and applied arts and sciences. The College is committed to an embracing evangelical spirit rooted in Anabaptist, Wesleyan, and Pietist traditions of the Christian church" (*About Messiah*, p. 1). This identity statement balances the liberal arts with professional programs in communicating institutional distinctiveness. The statement also confirms the germaneness of Messiah's theological heritage, as well as its commitment to ecumenism. The identity statement knit unity together from the diverse strands of institutional heritage (personal communication with R. J. Sawatsky, 2001).

The identity statement is coupled with the mission statement, "to educate men and women toward maturity of intellect, character, and Christian faith in preparation for lives of service, leadership, and reconciliation in church and society" (*About Messiah*, p. 1). The statement articulates intended outcomes for student learning and development, as well as a commitment to serve the larger world. The college is united by a commitment to serve the commons, in church and society. In its earliest days, service to the world took shape through ministry and missions. Although ministry and missions remain viable vocations for Messiah graduates, service to the world takes shape in scholarship, engineering, and public service as well.

Ernest Boyer had strong ties with Messiah, as well as significant influence over shaping and directing the college's mission. Boyer graduated from Messiah in 1948 and served the college for many years as a trustee. On the occasion of the college's seventy-fifth anniversary, Boyer (1984) delivered a convocation address titled "Retaining the Legacy of Messiah College." The legacy he articulated focused on an education that expands knowledge yet retains a commitment to campus community. The community-building efforts of Messiah College are nurtured by a shared commitment to educational mission.

Foundational Values

Five foundational values were outlined prior to the revision of the identity and mission statement. These remain core values of the college. In addition to the "significance of community," each of the four additional values underlines a distinctive understanding of the common ethos of the college. These values also profess the importance of community. The "importance of the person" emphasizes the value of each and every individual. The contributions of gender and ethnicity to the community are affirmed in this value. Each person has responsibility, as well as the freedom, to pursue truth and develop an academic course of study within their experience of Christian faith. The value, "unity of faith, learning, and life," affirms the wholeness of persons and a holistic notion of faith, intellect, and character. In addition, "disciplined and creative living" authenticates the role of community members as actors and interpreters of the world. Finally, "service and reconciliation" speaks directly to the intersection of justice and community. The calling to be agents of reconciliation to God, to persons, and to the world is a central assertion of the experience and intended outcomes of community for Messiah College. Service is a central means and expression of the work of reconciliation. Service both contributes to community and constructs it.

Building community at Messiah College is a direct extension of the mission, identity, and foundational values of the college itself. Being in community extends from our shared historical understandings of community and the narratives that in turn shape new understandings today.

Administrative Organization and Governance

Messiah College's commitment to institutional mission takes shape in college governance and administrative organization of the educational program. The holistic education of intellect, character, and faith requires cocurricular educational opportunities to augment classroom learning. Messiah's educational governance system is called the Community of Educators; membership includes faculty and out-of-class educators. The community's dialogue and the decisions they make address the content and fulfillment of educational objectives through both the curriculum and the cocurriculum.

Messiah College adopted a provost model for education in 1994. This model was instituted to facilitate the college's commitment to holistic education. The provost is responsible for the whole educational program and administers the efforts of the faculty, as well as educators in Student Affairs and College Ministries.

The provost model and the Community of Educators model do not insulate our institution from the challenges of bridging in-class and out-of-class education. The models do provide an avenue for reaching our articulated goals for holistic education. Their intention and potential lie in their direct relation to the pursuit of mission through the delivery of a seamless education. The increased size of the institution resulted in a major reorganization of the college's academic units. In July 2001, following a year of dialogue and decision making, thirteen academic departments were reorganized into five schools representing twenty academic departments. This reorganization provides yet a new opportunity amidst a dynamic institution to reshape a common experience of community. Students will connect with a school as part of their affiliation with the college.

Building Community Through Ethos Education

Mission and identity are essential to building community. A shared understanding of mission and core institutional values is nurtured by developing a common understanding of these commitments. Ethos education has been an important avenue toward building community at Messiah College.

Community Covenant

A central dimension of a disciplined community is nurturing the commitment of all community members to the common good (Boyer, 1990). The ethos statement of Messiah College titled "Our

Community Covenant" knits the college together by articulating common expectations for interpersonal relationships and practice in the college environment. The covenant outlines a balance between personal freedom and corporate responsibility; it articulates a commitment to searching for truth and promoting learning. The covenant outlines the central aspirations for Messiah College as a Christian academic community and addresses the general expectations of both students and employees. These expectations take unique expression for employees and students and are voiced in specific documents for these respective constituencies. The covenant provides a contextual framework for moral reflection and decision making and calls members to integrity as a core commitment to our community of learning.

A second component of a disciplined community is a set of clearly stated standards of behavior in both the civic and scholarly realms of campus life. The college has been intentional in developing and articulating mutual expectations between the institution and students. The college's governance system allows for the joint participation of faculty, student affairs educators, and students in the review and revision of campus standards. Review and revision occur in the context of the college's educational objectives.

The college has nurtured a disciplined community in an effort to foster a campus culture consistent with our educational mission. The covenant has been a meaningful document to the Messiah community since its adoption in 1983. As the college grew in size, the meaning of the covenant was less well understood and at times even misunderstood. Efforts to articulate the covenant and its purpose no longer fit the institutional environment. On recognizing these challenges, the Division of Student Affairs sought new avenues for reclaiming shared meaning for the covenant. As the college grew in size, it became apparent that beginning our educational efforts during matriculation was too late. Therefore, we worked to create an ethos of learning to ensure that students understand policies and standards upon their introduction to the community.

Realizing the full potential for building community begins the moment a prospective student visits the campus. Admissions counselors articulate the values of community and interpret the literature of Messiah College as they express the educational experiences prospective students can expect. Given the importance of the admissions process to orienting prospective members to community values, the covenant is integrated into admissions materials. Thus each prospective student can learn about the covenant through admissions literature. In open houses, parents of prospective students also learn about the covenant and are encouraged to discuss the document as their son or daughter completes the admissions application. A space on the application enables applicants to affirm their voluntary commitment to entering the community. The covenant provides a means for students to enter into the obligations and opportunities of community membership that accompany enrollment (*About Messiah*, pp. 21–24). Beginning our educational efforts during the admissions process has allowed students to commit to the obligations of the community as they commit to the opportunities afforded them through a Messiah education. The admissions process then sets in progress a seamless orientation process for incoming students.

Welcome Week

Matriculated students receive a comprehensive introduction to the college community through an expansive Welcome Week program. Welcome Week provides a holistic orientation to social, academic, and spiritual life on campus. Welcome Week includes a candlelight service, opening convocation, educational experiences on community and racial justice, social interaction, dialogues on common reading, and the year's first class sessions.

The candlelight service is an important ritual that affirms formal entry into the community. Students and their families participate in the service. The event underscores the commitment of the Messiah community to students and allows parents and educators to publicly declare their support for this class of students. Public affirmation of all constituencies has been an important ritual in building community.

On the first day of classes, a campuswide convocation provides the president an opportunity to welcome the incoming class and returning students to the community. Convocation celebrates excellent teachers through public recognition of Teaching Excellence Award recipients and the honoring of distinguished professors. Students who have exemplified outstanding service, academic achievement, and involvement are honored as Boyer Scholars.

Many programmatic elements of Welcome Week involve immersion into the community ethos. Incoming students participate in a half-day of service in the local community that engages students in the college's value of service. This initiative also facilitates college connections to the local community and has provided a foundation for ongoing college-community partnerships.

Incoming students also rotate through peer-facilitated educational sessions. Two of these sessions address community. Focusing on unity and diversity within our community, one session focuses on racial justice and cultural appreciation. Another session provides students a richer understanding of the central theological and educational themes of the covenant. Students reaffirm their commitment to the covenant through a corporate ritual of signing a copy of it to take with them. Upper-class students facilitate this session, as peer education communicates the shared commitment to the covenant. These sessions have created a better understanding among students of the covenant as a shared commitment. These peer-facilitated sessions have increased the critical mass of students who have an in-depth understanding of the covenant as well. This model has demonstrated a better fit with the current institutional size and environment. A peer education session on academic integrity is being planned for future years.

The programs that make up Welcome Week are merely one element of the educational contribution to community. The process by which these initiatives are formed and implemented also contributes to community. Purposefully designed peer groups are a cornerstone of the Welcome Week process. Peer groups are formed, based on students enrolled in each first-year seminar—a theme-based writing course that is part of Messiah's general education curriculum. A partnership between the Orientation and General Education departments shaped the selection process for upper-class students to serve as leaders for these peer groups. Campus educators nominate these peer leaders, who are selected for their ability to facilitate group process and also for excellent writing skills. Peer leaders participate in the Welcome Week program, assist in class for the first six weeks of the seminar, and provide out-of-class connections for seminar participants. The peer leaders and faculty are able to participate with their seminar participants in the Welcome Week service experience. As a result, faculty often recognize names and faces prior to the first day of class. This directly contributes to not only the experience of community-at-large but also the experience of these classrooms as communities of learning. This curricular and cocurricular partnership positively affects the development of the individual learning communities for first-year students.

Welcome Week is successful because of the involvement of faculty, out-of-class educators, student organizations, and campus leaders. While new students are introduced to the values of the community, the partnerships of the community itself are stretched and strengthened as hospitality is extended to new members.

Common Learning

The college environment is a critical element of educational community. In academic year 1999–2000, the college adopted a common learning theme to emphasize learning and reflection collegewide. Given the historical transition, the theme "People, Ideas and Machines: A Twentieth-Century Retrospective" was particularly appropriate. The introduction of the common learning theme provided a connective thread to several existing activities. Each of the residence halls provided passive education on the learning theme. Residence hall decor and fall events not typically viewed as relevant to learning contributed to the campuswide theme and thus to the learning environment itself. An annual event called Family Weekend took the theme, "We Are Family." The event advanced common understanding with a theme relevant both to the college theme and to the experiences of students' parents. The Student Handbook included notable quotes and college photographs from the twentieth century.

Developing connections among college experiences enriched our learning environment. The common learning themes helped connect the out-of-class curriculum, including lectures, theater productions, and the campus radio station and newspaper to the course-based curriculum. The intellectual, aesthetic, social, and spiritual dimensions of campus life are advanced through contribution to the whole. The common learning theme was an opportunity to capitalize on the potential afforded a residential college by integrating the learning environment.

Educational purposefulness and common learning are at the center of the curriculum. Specifically, general education is a venue for sustaining community. General education transforms students into citizens and transmits institutional "identity, meaning, values, and culture" (Bucher, 1999, p. 4). General education introduces all students to knowledge that the faculty of that institution has defined as essential. Students are provided interdisciplinary connections and encouraged to apply knowledge to their personal experience. Connections to self and others construct community. Examining general education through the lens of community provides a critical opportunity for colleges and universities to build community on campus and in society. Educational community in higher education frames vocation and shapes values.

Provost Seminar

Students are not the sole constituency for building community. A Provost Seminar was introduced at Messiah College in the Fall of 1997 to orient faculty and out-of-class educators to the mission, identity, and values of Messiah College. The weekly, semester-long seminar advances community on campus by orienting new members of the community who are responsible for advancing the mission both in and out of the classroom. Seminar content includes an overview of the theological heritage of the institution, an exploration of its mission and identity, and the realization of mission in educational programs.

The Provost Seminar has proven a crucial element of introducing educators to the heritage and educational foundations of the college. With few faculty representing the denomination, the seminar encourages an understanding of the Brethren-in-Christ theology. The seminar also communicates the importance of holistic learning and development in Messiah's educational objectives.

Cohort groups from the Provost Seminar also build a strong sense of community and camaraderie. Student Affairs educators and teaching faculty are able to build relationships that provide a foundation for educational partnerships.

Educator Development

The ongoing development of educational community depends on the professional growth and development of faculty and out-of-class educators. Relationships between teaching faculty and out-of-class educators provide space for a seamless implementation of education. Several initiatives have been instituted to enhance these relationships and the ongoing development of educators in recent years.

A monthly program titled "Chat-n-Chew" encourages excellence in teaching. This informal initiative encourages creative teaching by bringing campus educators together for conversations on teaching and learning. Seasoned as well as newer faculty have been able to share what they have learned about good teaching in our context. Sessions have addressed teaching techniques, learning environments, and ways to understand students. Each session provides opportunity for small-group dialogue and personal application. Chat-n-Chew sessions provide an opportunity for personal reflection and for building collegial relationships, as well as a time to shape individual and corporate educational practice.

Regular sessions titled "Scholarship Colloquies" have encouraged excellence in scholarship and furthered a shared understanding of scholarship in our particular context. Part of the theological heritage of the institution places a unique emphasis on scholarship of engagement and practice. The integration of faith and learning is critical, as is the understanding of faith in practice. A senior faculty member supports this ongoing initiative in which campus educators read current and classic texts that apply to scholarship. Dialogue about the text and its application furthers a shared understanding of scholarship, encourages shared ideas, and challenges assumptions.

Building Community Through Partnership

Community on campus is centered on mission and depends on an understanding of the distinct expression of community by its members. Programs shaped by educational partnerships sustain community. Community is enriched as students become engaged members of a community of learning.

Residence-Based Academic Learning Community

In the fall of 2000, the college piloted a residence-based academic learning community. Both the outcome and the process required a partnership between the offices of Academic Affairs and Student Affairs on campus.

Academic and Student Affairs leaders considered learning community models. Examining the literature on academic learning communities, as well as researching other institutional models, provided opportunities to understand both the contribution and the potential pitfalls in the development and implementation of the program.

The hope was to design a learning community uniquely pertinent to the college's mission and identity. The partnership was designed to meet the educational objectives of the college. The resulting pilot program, titled "The Christian Imagination," involved thirty-two students in a learning community. The purpose of the pilot was to strengthen connections between curricular learning and cocurricular experiences, increase student engagement, enhance the intellectual atmosphere of the residence hall, and help students make connections among fields of knowledge. All thirty-two students were assigned to two residence hall floors devoted to the pilot and enrolled in the same General Education course titled "Introduction to the Bible." Half of the students were assigned to a first-year seminar section on faith and the visual arts; the other half were assigned to a first-year seminar on faith and literature.

This living-learning community created some strong community experiences for participating learners and teachers. Program assessment included feedback from residence education personnel and faculty. Community engagement outcome comparisons were made for students involved in the learning community and those in similar courses without the learning community component. Classroom engagement was also assessed.

Early assessment data have not indicated a strong difference in how students perceive their relationships with faculty. Faculty feedback indicates that students were generally more engaged in class discussion and that relationships outside the classroom generally enhanced course conversation. The weaknesses of the first year of the pilot were in the out-of-class programs that did not meet student expectations. The pilot has continued for a second year. The extension of the pilot has allowed us to assess potential as well as real outcomes, as we consider the future of the program.

Wittenburg Door

An open community balances personal freedom with corporate responsibility. Open dialogue is critical to educational community. A mutually open and caring community considers the merits of the opposing viewpoint and affirms the other in spite of disagreement.

Essentially, community is sustained by a campus climate that honors relationships and care in the context of vigorous pursuit of truth.

The Messiah College student government encourages this discourse through the Wittenburg Door—a public space in the Campus Center that encourages members of the community to post their opinions. Students post their ideas and questions about the college community, current societal events, and international concerns. Other members of the community are encouraged to respond and continue the dialogue. Students, educators, staff, and administrators are often found gathered around the Wittenburg Door, discussing issues of importance to the community. These verbal exchanges advance the dialogue of the Wittenburg Door.

The Wittenburg Door has emulated the many challenges of open community. The initiative began as an actual wooden door on which notes were posted. This door has been removed from the center twice. The responsible parties communicated anonymously to the student government that the door was not being administered responsibly. It was absent from the campus for two years. A senior proposed its reestablishment. The student government association spent a semester engaged in conversation about the parameters for its return. The Wittenburg Door today exists as a bulletin board in the Campus Center with distinct categories of feedback: campus, country, and international concerns. The Wittenburg Door remains a delicate balance between personal freedom of expression and care for others. The debate is often heated, whether about campus issues, government policy, or global poverty. Open community is a difficult challenge for college administrators and for students; this has been evident in the Wittenburg Door at Messiah College.

Micah Partnership for Racial Justice and Multicultural Education

The essence of a just community is predicated on two mutual ideas—the sacredness of each individual and the value of pluralism. Strengthening campus community involves commitment to individual gifts as well as a diverse commons. Messiah College has committed itself to equality of opportunity by establishing goals for enrollment along with a commitment to the success of students of color. As efforts have failed and succeeded and lessons have been learned, the college has paused at various times to confirm its commitment and reassess necessary efforts to fulfill this commitment.

Recognizing a need to reaffirm our commitment to holistic efforts toward just community, the Micah Partnership for Racial Justice and Multicultural Education was formed in 1998. Messiah College instituted the Micah Partnership to advance our identity as a just community. This is part of Messiah's institutional efforts to "add more pluralistic dimensions to our understanding of and practice of community" (Bucher, 1999, p. 17). Theologically, the partnership of faculty, students, administrators, and staff centers on the sacredness of each person and the Christian calling to be ambassadors of reconciliation. Racial justice focuses on underlying systemic challenges on campus and in our world. Multicultural education focuses on the appreciation of difference. A foundation of the Micah Partnership is that racial justice and multicultural education must occur concurrently for authentic reconciliation to be realized.

Accomplishments of the Micah Partnership include the development and approval of policy and response protocol for incidents of racism on campus. The policy and protocol were constructed to connect with theological foundations, mission, and college governance. The distinct application of curricular and cocurricular learning environments was also incorporated.

Challenges in the partnership have been many. This has been difficult work both emotionally and intellectually. The balance of short- and long-term goals that sustain energy as well as demonstrate real progress has been tenuous. Four years at a college is a small portion of the experience for most employees. For students, these four years are the whole of their experience. The work of racial justice and multicultural education must not only transform the larger campus climate but must address the specific needs of currently enrolled students of color. We have learned many lessons. We have valued the contribution of an external consultant in guiding our work and decision making. The most important lesson has been that the relationships within the partnership create space for bridging understanding across cultures and are the foundation of ongoing progress.

Multicultural Council

One avenue of college support for students of color has been the formation of the Multicultural Council. The council was formed as a part of student government to build collaboration among student organizations that advance the goals of a diverse community. The council provides collective representation of several student groups. The integration of leadership of the council provides a strong voice at the student government leadership table. An elected student government leader has responsibility to chair and maintain the involvement of the council in student governance.

The individual organizations maintain their distinct ethos and focus on supporting a particular population of students. Phi Omega Chi (People of Color United for Christ) was the first student organization at Messiah that was founded to support students of color. La Alianzia Latina and the Asian Student Fellowship were developed in recent years to support these student populations. The International Student and Mu Kappa Association supports international students and children of international missionaries. In addition to these organizations, two residence units have formed in recent years on campus. The Unity and Perspectives Floor is a thematic residence community in which students have a roommate from a different culture and participate in activities that advance cultural awareness. The Rafiki House is a theme-based residence house for international students.

Each of these organizations, individually and collectively, provide support to individual students and contribute events that educate the community. Student organizations and the Multicultural Council are critical partners with administrative offices in the advancement of a campus learning environment that supports cultural appreciation. Our international student community invigorates our campus by celebrating the many cultures among us. The Office of College Ministries, in collaboration with student organizations, coordinates Tapestry Week—a campuswide theme week focused on multicultural awareness. Tapestry Week activities have included a film series, speakers, discussion groups, and student art shows.

Agape Center for Service and Learning

The essence of caring community is that service is encouraged (Boyer, 1990). Agape, a Greek word for love, communicates the foundation of care that is at the core of service. Messiah College develops the mind, heart, and soul, as well as the commitment to use these to serve the commons. Community is advanced as individuals see themselves as part of something larger than themselves.

The Agape Center for Service and Learning was founded at Messiah in 1998 to enable students to channel their intellect toward service. The Agape Center develops collaboration among students, faculty, and members of the community who have a common interest in service and learning. The center brings together administrative offices focused on community service, service learning, and missions, as well as student organizations with similar foci. The partnership provides a central, interactive place for the coordination of local and global service initiatives. The center enables the college to be intentional in building reciprocal partnerships with community agencies and to ensure excellent praxis in service education. The Agape Center provides a community within the community that advances the goals of service and shapes the practice and understanding of service within the college community.

Service Day is an institutionwide initiative coordinated by the Agape Center during Spring term. Service Day is built into the college calendar; classes do not meet, and most administrative offices close. On Service Day 2000, over 62 percent of the eligible student population participated; faculty, administrators, and staff participated as well. In addition to hosting one thousand Special Olympians for their spring games, over forty different local community service agencies were served. Campus administrators, to express thanks, served lunch to local fire and law enforcement agencies. Multiple campus and community partnerships were necessary to the implementation of Service Day. The human and financial resources dedicated to the success of Service Day indicate a strong corporate commitment to community.

Reclaiming Community Through Celebration

A celebrative community remembers institutional heritage. A celebrative community shares rituals and traditions that connect individuals to the campus and its history. Rites, ceremonies, and celebrations unite the campus and provide students a sense of belonging in something meaningful and enduring. The development and sustaining of campus traditions at Messiah has been challenged by campus growth. Maintaining a strong commitment to institutional heritage and also advancing contemporary expressions of community has been critical.

Koinonia Week

In spring 2001, the Division of Student Affairs initiated a theme week to renew and advance our collective understanding of and commitment to community. Representatives of the student government were enthusiastic about the idea but recommended we not title the event "Community Week." Ironically, students felt *community* was an overused term that had lost meaning. The title "Koinonia," which is the Greek word for fellowship or community, was then chosen. Koinonia Week provided an opportunity to reflect on what uniquely defines our community and how we might faithfully pursue that vision.

Koinonia Week 2001 was planned to coincide with several existing expressions of community, including Service Day, Messiah theater, the Messiah Choral Arts Society concert, several intercollegiate athletic events, and the annual Athletics Banquet. The student government planned their annual banquet to coincide with Koinonia Week. The college's 2001 Solar Car, Genesis, was unveiled on campus. A weekly common chapel kicked off the celebration by focusing on community. A dessert celebration following Service Day allowed students to document their reflections on large bulletin boards. These bulletin boards were displayed throughout the remainder of the week. Each initiative was shaped to uniquely highlight the contribution to community.

The inclusion of athletics in Koinonia Week highlighted their contribution to community spirit on campus. Students, employees, and alumni are united behind a common passion for Messiah athletics. Camaraderie is evident in the stands and on the field. In 2000, the Music Department formed a college pep band that has contributed to community spirit and celebration at athletic events.

Koinonia Week celebrated both tradition and innovation. The planning partners for Koinonia Week include representatives from each of the class councils. Even prior to implementing the first Koinonia Week, students, faculty, and employees anticipated the celebration becoming an annual spring tradition. Koinonia Week has been incorporated into existing student governance structures. This event will continue on an annual basis, allowing us to pause and celebrate who we are every year. New ideas for sustaining Koinonia Week in the future include a Scholarship Showcase, where students can publicly share their academic work, as well as photo collages illustrating the lives of members of the Messiah Community.

Reflections and Application

Messiah College is in many ways unique as a faith-based, residential, undergraduate college. Nonetheless, the lessons for building community are applicable in diverse institutional contexts. Every institution of higher education has a unique purpose that led to its founding. This purpose remains the central narrative of the institution over time, even as the mission is reshaped and rearticulated in light of the environment. This mission is the cornerstone of community. Composing a common community experience begins with creating a common understanding of mission.

Building community requires implementing the values and practices of community in concrete ways. Messiah College leaders have learned to recognize ongoing, existing programs and practices for their contribution to campus community. Examining current rhetoric, programs, and practice through the lens of community has supported our efforts. Several of the initiatives outlined in this chapter were not developed with the idea of building community but were nonetheless expressions of campus community and values. One lesson Messiah College can provide for other institutions is to examine current programs and practice for community prior to developing new initiatives. An informal environmental scan provides a baseline for community efforts. Claiming these efforts as expressions of community is a valuable task for an institution. Viewing these initiatives collectively provides a foundation for the assessment of current programs and direction for the development of new initiatives. Examining current programs for their underlying values offers an opportunity to examine what is communicated regarding community on campus. It is an opportunity to discern espoused values that are not fully and intentionally advanced.

Boyer (1990, p. 3) asked: "If the college cannot come together in a shared vision of its central mission, how can we hope to sustain community in society at large?" The ability to create community in a dynamic society is at stake, as each institution builds community that connects to its distinctive mission.

Two central lessons are offered by Messiah College: (1) community efforts must be centered in institutional mission and (2) mission is fulfilled through building campus community.

References

About Messiah. [brochure]. Grantham, PA: Messiah College Press.

Brensinger, T. (2000). *Focusing our faith: Brethren in Christ core values*. Nappanee, IN: Evangel Publishing Company.

Boyer, E. L. (1984). Retaining the legacy of Messiah College. Address delivered at Messiah College. In *About Messiah*, Grantham, PA: Messiah College Press.

Boyer, E. L. (1990). *Campus life: In search of community*. San Francisco: The Carnegie Foundation for the Advancement of Teaching.

Bucher, G. (1999). The new quest for common learning: Boyer, Berkeley, Bloom, and beyond. Address delivered at Messiah College.

Palmer, P. (1999). The recovery of community in higher education: Focus on teaching and learning. Address delivered at Messiah College.

Sider, E. M. (1984). *Messiah College: A history*. Nappanee, IN.

4

Modeling Community Through Campus Leadership

Larry D. Roper and Susan D. Longerbeam

This chapter guides the reader through the creation and implementation of the Campus Compact by the Division of Student Affairs at Oregon State University. The following story will include our successes and failures, struggles and achievements, and present to the reader at least one possible approach to leadership in the context of a college or university environment.

Understanding Leadership Context

Oregon State University is a state-supported land-grant institution. The university is situated in a predominantly white community with a population of 50,000. At the time this leadership initiative was launched in 1995, we had an enrollment of approximately 12,500 students—10 percent from racial and ethnic minority groups (Asian and Pacific Americans, Chicano and Latino and Mexican Americans, American Indians, and African Americans); 12 percent were international. About 20 percent of the students were graduate students, primarily in the sciences. Fewer than 5 percent of our faculty is classified as belonging to racial or ethnic minorities.

The Division of Student Affairs comprises Housing and Dining Services, Student Health Services, Recreational Sports, Memorial Union, Student Media, Student Involvement (Diversity Development, Greek Life, Women's Development, and Student

Organizations), Counseling and Psychological Services, Career Services, Services for Students with Disabilities, Student Conduct, Minority Education Offices (one for each of the four ethnic groups listed), and the Educational Opportunities Program. The Division of Student Affairs has more than four hundred full-time employees. More than six thousand students live in university-supervised and approved housing.

In 1995, the university was in the midst of several years of successive budget cuts and a ten-year declining enrollment trend. The Division of Student Affairs, like much of the university, exhibited what can best be described as "at-risk" behaviors. Generally, the staff members showed an absence of hope for the future; there appeared to be an inability to engage in trusting relationships; there was widespread isolation within Student Affairs units; and there appeared to be an unwillingness to take risks on behalf of themselves or others. These behaviors arose because of—and may be partially attributable to—a series of dramatic budget cuts that resulted in massive staff decreases and program reductions.

The challenge that confronted Student Affairs was to produce leadership within our staff that would allow us to exhibit the attributes of a confident, connected, productive, visionary, proactive, and hopeful organization.

A mix of social and institutional agendas was both directly and indirectly influencing the environment in which Student Affairs was functioning, though not all were related. Among the predominant issues were

- An institutional priority to increase the diversity of our staff and student body

- An articulated goal of increasing student enrollment

- A 28 percent attrition rate for first-year students

- Overt competition among university staff for institutional resources

Issues beyond the university included

- A volatile political environment in which taxpayers had for several years voted to reduce funding to the state government and state-supported institutions of higher education

- A swing of political conservatism that resulted in a number of ballot measures that created angry public debate

- The occurrence of a few high-profile hate crimes in the state

Adopting a Leadership Model

The department heads of all Student Affairs units met on a bi-weekly basis and attempted to function as a leadership body for the Student Affairs organization. However, the group struggled greatly to define a vision, develop teamlike relationships, and identify essential leadership activities that would construct a clear destination for the organization. The struggle was not successful. After a number of discussions about possible approaches to achieving engagement and alignment, the department heads agreed that the vice provost should open the leadership and visioning process to others in the division beyond the department heads group.

The department heads had previously agreed that the most compelling principles on which to base our efforts was the work of Ernest Boyer. The department heads agreed that the principles outlined by Boyer in *Campus Life: In Search of Community* (1990) were the most promising foundation on which to build our future. With the goal of creating engaged, broad-based leadership, in February 1996 the vice provost for student affairs sent a "Dear Colleague" letter to all four hundred employees in our Student Affairs organization. The letter offered everyone the opportunity to participate in a process to define the direction of our organization's leadership. The invitation to participate specified that a group was being convened to develop a Campus Compact.

Ernest Boyer (1990) offered the term *campus compact* to describe leadership action that he believed was essential to advance campus community. In Boyer's words, "The president may wish to convene a campus-wide forum, or use existing forums . . . . to discuss the six principles and the idea of adopting them, more formally, as a campus *compact*." Boyer further states, "To adopt the principles as a campus compact would signal the seriousness with which the enduring values of the institution were understood and embraced" (pp. 65–66).

The condition of our institution was such that a campuswide conversation at this time was not feasible. As we were beginning this effort, our institution was undergoing a leadership transition; we were searching for a new president.

Our challenge at this time was to initiate a process that was responsive to the institutional climate while also acknowledging our own organizational challenges. The process that we designed seemed to account for the climate within our university and organization.

The initial charge to Student Affairs, contained in the letter from the vice provost, read: "The Compact will identify standards of service, values, and activities we will initiate to achieve the principles of community and make clear the contributions we intend to make to Oregon State University."

To ensure that involvement was open to everyone, supervisors were instructed that they could not restrict employee involvement in the process; participation was to be open to any interested employee. The letter related the struggle previously described in the chapter and our frustration with being unable to determine what our contributions should be to the strategic direction of the university. Our previous discussions revealed to us that other important voices were not included in the conversations. As a result, we extended an invitation to others to become involved. The discussions also revealed that the creativity and energy level among department heads was very low; they could not lead in the way our organization required. Involving others felt like the only hope we had for moving our organization forward.

The invitation to participate said that we would use the work of Ernest Boyer as the framework for our discussions but that those who became involved in the process would determine the particular direction of our efforts. Participants were advised that the process would involve an undefined number of meetings. The only stipulations placed on involvement were that participants must possess positive energy and must have a tolerance for ambiguity. Our belief was (and is) that our organization, as is the case with any organization, cannot afford to be led by people who are tired.

The process was designed to be voluntary; no person in Student Affairs was required to participate. We believed it was essential that those with energy should construct our future. At that stage in our organization's development, we were not inclined to expend our energy attempting to convince those involved in the conversation that we needed to rethink our connection to the university's mission, the relationship of student affairs to the academic program, and the relationship of individual departments with each other. We needed those who were already committed to new thinking to perform the leadership in this critical process.

Because participation was optional, several department heads chose not to be involved, and we agreed to not make judgments about those who chose not to participate. We also agreed that everyone would support whatever direction the group defined as our destination. At the core of our agreement was a decision that department heads would honor the work produced through the divisionwide leadership effort. It was understood that at no point would any of the ideas or initiatives generated by the group be brought back to the department heads for approval. In essence, we agreed that we would not take ideas that were created through an organic leadership process and subject them to a hierarchical decision-making structure. The conversation about honoring energy over position proved to be crucial to our future development and now serves as one of the cornerstones of our leadership philosophy. The Campus Compact process was moved forward to the broader student affairs organization by a small group of department heads and the vice provost.

Designing Organizational Conversations

A conversation model was used to construct the leadership agenda for the Division of Student Affairs at Oregon State University. Approximately seventy-five staff members attended the initial conversation that we convened to construct a new leadership culture. Those who were involved represented a broad cross-section of job types, education levels, and length of employment at the university. The vice provost for student affairs, who began by setting the context for the conversations, facilitated the process.

Part of the context setting provided clarification about the focus for the subsequent conversations. The specific focus of our work centered on two activities. We first answered two questions; then we constructed leadership activities in response to those questions. The stimulus questions were: What will be our contribution to the mission of Oregon State University? and What does the university most need from us right now?

In preparation for the conversation, all members of the Division of Student Affairs were provided access to the work of Ernest Boyer in the form of books and texts of his speeches on community. Almost all participants had read or conversed about Boyer's work with colleagues prior to entering the conversation. Our conversations took place in two-hour time blocks and were held in large rooms that were conducive to face-to-face interaction, as well as breakout conversations.

Participants began by generating a set of ground rules to guide the process, which was important because it helped create a design for collegial relationships. In addition, the ideas offered by group members enhanced participants' awareness of what their colleagues needed from them in order to feel safe in a creative process. As we got deeper into the process, a number of participants reflected on the ground rules activity as a significant act. It was the first time that some had ever heard from their colleagues that they were willing to honor them as peers. The ground rules provided a general design for creating and sustaining equal-status relationships.

Second, the group moved to discuss the principles of community included in the Boyer documents that we were using (purposeful, open, just, disciplined, caring, celebrative). We then defined what each principle meant to us by developing our own operational definitions for each of the six principles. This was an important stage because it allowed colleagues who had very little awareness of each other's values and perspectives to develop a shared understanding of the principles on which our professional work would be grounded. This activity also proved to be important for generating excitement for the work ahead of us. As we discussed the Boyer principles, a sense of hope began to permeate the group.

During the second conversation session, the group endorsed a suggestion made by one of the participants that we follow the lead of Ernest Boyer and make the focus of our work to develop a Campus Compact. Though Boyer's recommendation was that the institution's president should lead the effort, members of the Division of Student Affairs believed that we had a responsibility to bring campuswide leadership to our colleagues across the university. At that point in our institution's life, we perceived a significant leadership void on campus. The outcome of our conversation was an explicit articulation that our motivation was to fill the void with positive energy and principle-based, value-added activities. We also believed that Student Affairs was the only entity that could enrich the humanity of the community at that time.

Our next step involved describing and visioning what the campus would look like if each principle were realized and what behaviors and dynamics would characterize a campus where the principles had not been realized. The visioning activity was important because it helped us focus on our preferred futures. As an organization, we began to function based on the possibilities that we saw for ourselves. Visioning activities are essential to inspiring creativity, taking risks, and making behavioral shifts. At Oregon State University, it was imperative that we move staff to a position of considering a way of life that would reduce isolation, enhance productivity, focus energy, and shift the conversation from the sources of misery to sources of hope.

Visioning set the stage for the group to begin considering our beliefs about the context in which we were doing our work. We believed it was important for us to identify our underlying values and assumptions about our university and our professional work because those beliefs would influence and guide us in our future activities. This conversation served to ground us and give clarity to our work and relationships.

The most important aspect of our conversation focused on deciding between the use of two simple words—*the* and *our*. In the end, this conversation was pivotal in the development of an organizational mind-set. The conversation centered on whether to refer to "the university" or "our university." Through our conversation, we concluded that it was imperative that we declare ownership for our institution and that we develop a leadership style that would reinforce this commitment.

The language that we used sent a powerful message about our relationship to Oregon State University, its members, and its mission. The assumptions that we outlined and subsequently included in *Campus Compact: A Statement of Vision, Values and Commitments* (Division of Student Affairs, 1997) are as follows (the first sentence became our mission statement):

> Student Affairs faculty and staff will provide leadership
> for the development of a positive sense of community at

Oregon State University. We will collaborate with others to enhance the educational environment and to support the teaching and learning process. We value and respect the individual and believe that sharing knowledge changes lives.

1. Our university is an environment where teaching and learning are the most important activities, and where challenge and support foster lifelong learning.
2. Our university is a learning community where there is respectful discourse, and a safe environment for taking risks, and where individuals and ideas can make a difference.
3. Our university is a network of relationships built upon shared responsibility and leadership, where community members work for common goals.
4. Our university is a community where we are empowered by the depth of our commonalities and strengthened by the affirmation of our individuality.
5. Our university is a dynamic, evolving environment where energy is intentionally focused toward sustaining and developing members.
6. Our university is an honest community where we are truthful about our struggles, acknowledge conflict, confront obstacles, and provide an environment for dialogue, discovery, and individual growth.
7. Our university is a place where we have pride in our traditions, hope for our future, and a commitment to progress and positive change.

Our university will achieve this vision only as the result of intentional actions on the part of campus community

members. We will develop a dynamic CAMPUS COM-
PACT, which will define our specific designed outcomes
and the actions through which we will accomplish them.
Our Compact is our pledge that we will move beyond
lofty ideas and engage in focused behavior [Division of
Student Affairs, 1997, pp. 1–2].

At each stage of the process, a group of volunteers worked to
edit and add focus to the work done in the large group conversations. The role of the vice provost, as facilitator of the process, was
to type and disseminate to participants all information generated at
each Campus Compact meeting. The small groups also functioned
as a form of team building, as they brought together diverse staff
from different departments to produce work on behalf of our organization. Eventually, this model would come to define the way
significant organizational change would be accomplished in the Student Affairs organization.

Putting Boyer's Principles at the Center

From the beginning of our conversations, even when our department heads group struggled to find some semblance of engagement
and balance, the work of Ernest Boyer rose to the top as the most
compelling principles on which to base our work. Although our direction was unclear, our communication disjointed, and energy random, our attraction was in one direction—toward the principles of
community outlined by Ernest Boyer. The idea of being a purposeful, open, just, disciplined, caring, and celebrative organization was
a very attractive prospect to a group that had suffered under budget
cuts, staff reductions, and program elimination.

When the group began its work, a surge of energy arose when
the members began discussing each of the principles. Although it
would have been easy to adopt the definitions Boyer created, our
organizational focus was aided by challenging ourselves to describe

what each of the principles meant to us. The depths of our commitment to the principles and the heights of our aspirations were raised by the standards that we set in constructing the definitions of the community principles.

The definitions, as created by members of the Campus Compact group (Division of Student Affairs, 1997, p. 3), are as follows:

> *Purposeful*—We aspire to create a purposeful community, dedicated to enabling individuals to be successful learners, teachers, and leaders in the University and in the larger community.
>
> *Open*—We aspire to create an open community where people feel safe to ask questions, to share ideas and experiences, and to express their individuality.
>
> *Just*—We aspire to create a just community, where the dignity of every individual is affirmed and where equality of opportunity is vigorously pursued.
>
> *Disciplined*—We aspire to create a disciplined community, where each member of the community is committed and responsible for upholding the standards and expectations conducive to the common good.
>
> *Caring*—We aspire to create a caring community where members value, nurture, respect and embrace each other, and where they take responsibility for the well-being of others.
>
> *Celebrative*—We aspire to create a celebrative community where we joyfully affirm all members and their contributions as meaningful to the University and the larger community.

Eventually, we reached the point where we had a clear vision and a statement of values, but we had not translated either the vision or values into specific actions. At this point, we brainstormed a list of *specific* behaviors and activities that we could pursue in order to achieve each of the six principles. By the end of this phase, we had over one hundred ideas for activities that we could pursue. Our final challenge was to identify the most significant issues to address in order to move Student Affairs and the university forward.

Designing Initiatives

Our work on identifying initiatives ultimately boiled down to the two questions mentioned earlier: For what are we willing to be held accountable? and What does the University most need from us right now? These questions forced us to think about how to be responsive to the needs and condition of the university while defining what we were willing to "own" as our issues. After significant discussion, we identified five areas of most immediate need: to provide support for the *Transition* needs of new students, to enhance the *Learning Environment*, to strengthen the *Cocurriculum*, to provide comprehensive *Professional Development*, and to implement focused, ongoing *Assessment*.

The descriptions for each of the initiatives, as included in the Campus Compact (Division of Student Affairs, 1997, pp. 4–5) are as follows:

> Support for *Student Transition Needs.* To work in a more focused way with students to assist them in their transition into the University and continue until graduation (or until their educational objectives have been attained) and into the entry level of their careers. We will pay special attention to first-year success, the need for academic support, and timely career advising.
>
> Enhancement of the *Learning Environment.* To create a "safe" learning environment to support student success, while offering opportunities to exchange ideas on important social issues. We will pay special attention to the physical settings in which learning takes place.

This may include focus on those factors that cause learners to feel "at risk" in certain settings.

Strengthen the *Co-Curriculum*. To strengthen the formal co-curriculum by coordinating more vigorously and setting more clear and specific expectations for Student Affairs staff involvement in facilitating students' experiences.

Comprehensive *Professional Development*. To prepare staff to be career-long learners, to acquire the knowledge and skills necessary to promote student growth, and to advance the Initiatives of the Compact. We will establish clear proficiency standards for staff performance and clear articulation of staff members' rights and responsibilities.

Focused, On-going *Assessment*. To implement a comprehensive, on-going assessment program to measure student and staff perceptions, assess needs, and establish baselines for staff performance and Student Affairs service.

Through the initiative process, we reconstructed relationships among those in Student Affairs and with colleagues across the campus. In addition, we developed focus for the work we would do, and we established accountability. At each stage of the process, we asked questions about which departments or individuals we needed to have relationships with in order to achieve success and also what learning and growth we needed to achieve in order to be successful.

For each initiative, we convened conversations with Student Affairs colleagues and colleagues from outside the division. Specifically, we invited our academic colleagues to join us in advancing those initiatives that were of shared concern. We had varying degrees of success with each initiative. In general, the clarity of the desired outcome most influenced our success.

In the final analysis, we evaluated three of the five initiatives as producing successful outcomes: Transitions, Assessment, and Professional Development.

Establishing Partnerships and Creating Teams

The Transitions initiative began with a conversation among Student Affairs colleagues, during which we created a clear vision of our desired outcomes. The specific outcome that we defined was the creation of a new, comprehensive student orientation program. During our conversations, we became aware that our academic colleagues had been meeting to consider ways to enhance student success and retention. With our goals in mind and an awareness of their interests, we convened a conversation with academic colleagues (in our university, orientation is structurally a part of Academic Affairs) to initiate a partnership. The result of this outreach gesture was the creation of a campuswide Transitions group that was cochaired by academic and Student Affairs colleagues. This leadership model produced several unprecedented programs and activities for our campus. Among them were

- A new student orientation program, which we named CONNECT

- The First-Year Experience program

- A preorientation, outdoor experience program

- Campuswide engagement of academic and student support units and athletics into an integrated program

- The development of operational definitions of a "well-oriented student" and "a university that orients students well"

- Integration of the local business and service community

The definitions of "a well-oriented student" and "a university that orients students well" were developed by the Transitions group as a way of giving clarity to the aspirations of the new student orientation program and identifying the kinds of institutional behaviors needed to stimulate greater educational success.

A specific example of a new organizational behavior that emerged from shared academic and student affairs leadership in Transitions was the use of the RFP (request for proposals) process to create alignment among orientation activities. This process required any campus unit wishing to offer activities during orientation week to respond to an RFP that defined the specific goals of the activity and how it would promote the development of "a well-oriented student."

Boyer's principles were integrated as the central theme in our orientation of new students. As part of our new student convocation, student leaders spoke about each of the principles and how they experienced them at Oregon State University; the vice provost for student affairs provided an overview of why the principles are important to our campus community. The principles were also used as an organizing framework to design classroom environments for our First-Year Experience course.

The Assessment and Professional Development initiatives also produced positive and lasting outcomes in response to the questions For what are we willing to be held accountable? and What does the university most need from us right now? The Professional Development group launched a number of divisionwide learning opportunities. Like the other initiatives, this effort was extended to include colleagues from outside of student affairs. The most significant effort of the Professional Development group was the leadership they provided to develop a Rights and Responsibilities document. This document is included as part of the Campus Compact and engaged all members of our Student Affairs organization in its creation.

The process by which the Rights and Responsibilities document was created was a series of unit-level conversations that were facilitated by Student Affairs colleagues from outside those units. The information gained through these conversations was compiled and sorted by members of the Professional Development group. The questions that drove the process and some of the important philosophical and behavioral commitments that emerged from the conversations are reflected in the following excerpt from the Campus Compact:

Rights and Responsibilities
An Initiative of the Campus Compact
Introduction

In the spring of 1996 members of the Division of Student Affairs at Oregon State University adopted the *Campus Compact*, a document in which we describe our aspirations to build a strong sense of community on the OSU campus. The Compact focuses on relationships, attitudes, and behavior we will foster throughout the University campus.

In the Compact we also identify specific initiatives through which we will achieve our desired outcomes. One of the initiatives, under the heading "Professional Development," focuses on enhancing personal growth and development of staff, establishing learning and performance expectations, and setting standards for professional relationships and service delivery. This document describes our goals and expectations.

The thoughts expressed in this document were generated through discussions among members of Student Affairs units, all of whom had the opportunity to be involved. Each work group responded to the following questions:

1. What do you feel are your basic rights as a member of the Student Affairs staff?
2. What responsibilities do you have to other members of the Student Affairs staff?

3. What are you willing to personally be held accountable for?
4. What responsibilities do your department, the Division of Student Affairs, and the University have to you?

The answers to these questions form the basis of our Rights and Responsibilities document.

This document does not replace job descriptions, union contracts, or other pre-existing documents. Nor is it meant to diminish our responsibility to meet all legal obligations for accessibility or other workplace standards. This is not a legal document. This is a document rooted in care—how we would like to be cared for, how we will care for our colleagues, and how we will show our care for OSU and its mission. This represents our best thinking about how we will approach our relationships with each other and how we will construct our work lives and relationships. The words and ideas expressed are those of the people who are employed in the Division of Student Affairs at Oregon State University. This document will serve as the standard toward which we aspire. Each work group will develop a specific plan for how to achieve this standard. Each will outline a regular process for evaluating their progress and achievements.

Our Basic Rights and Responsibilities
We want a work environment characterized by open and honest communication, where members show respect for the needs, interests, concerns, challenges, and humanity of co-workers. We will accept responsibility for fostering relationships of appreciation, recognition, support, celebration, and commitment to each other's well-being and success. Positive treatment and care will be accorded to all because it is our responsibility to acknowledge the

dignity of each person, not simply that person's perceived status. We will be committed to doing a good job and acting in good faith on behalf of ourselves, students, our units, our Division, the University, and the taxpayers of the state of Oregon. Above all else, we will practice respect, open communication, and creating an enriching work environment for all members [Division of Student Affairs, 1997, pp. 8–9].

The process of developing the Rights and Responsibilities document created increased focus for our relationship expectations and a design for constructing a professionally supportive environment; it also provided a barometer for measuring our progress toward the desired relationships. An important consideration in the final editing of the Rights and Responsibilities document was ensuring that the language used honored and reflected the words offered by our colleagues in their unit discussions. The Rights and Responsibilities document is written in the voice of our Student Affairs colleagues.

The work of the Professional Development group served to create relationship alignment within the Division of Student Affairs. By leading us to develop the Rights and Responsibilities document, the group helped us construct a relationship ethos and offered us language that is used by our members daily to remind each other of the standard that we have articulated.

The Assessment group began as a conversation among Student Affairs colleagues and eventually broadened to include colleagues from academic affairs. This initiative provided us with a number of lasting effects: a brochure that outlines best practices in assessment, a consultation team model that works with members of our organization and informs unit-level assessment efforts, generation of universitywide assessment data and efforts, and a bridge to the creation of a university institutional research office. Prior to this group's work, little was done in the area of assessment at our university. As a result of their efforts, consciousness has been raised and activity has been generated across the campus. Most recently, the vice president for finance and administration asked this group to develop position descriptions and produce a design for an Office of Institutional Research. This occurred because our organization has constructed an assessment knowledge base that is seen as valuable by other colleagues.

What Didn't Work

Although we experienced a great deal of success with Transitions, Professional Development, and Assessment initiatives, we were much less successful with Co-Curriculum and Learning Environment. Both of these initiatives are examples of what happens when members of an organization fail to free themselves of tradition, comfort, and unproductive structures. Through conversation, we concluded that the initiatives that failed did so because of applying rigid leadership approaches that were not appropriate for activities that relied on grassroots efforts and volunteer energy. In the cases where we were not successful, it was clear that those involved tried to force an organic process to fit into the previously existing rigid structure. The individuals who served as conveners for those initiatives attempted to fit the initiatives to the styles of leadership most accessible to them. All of our initiatives required that we invent new styles to achieve our desired results.

Prior to beginning the Campus Compact process, some members of the Student Affairs organization had attempted to implement a cocurricular transcript. The individuals involved with the cocurricular transcript effort who were involved with the formation of the Compact saw the Compact as a vehicle through which they could revive a failed effort. As we were deciding which initiatives to launch, there was enough support for a cocurricular initiative that it was included in our leadership agenda. Unfortunately, the leaders failed to involve members of the group in the creation of a new initiative. The group was managed as if it were a committee and was asked to resurrect old work for which they had no energy. The members eventually disengaged and the effort failed.

The Learning Environment initiative was broad, vague, and not measurable. Though the value of contributing to the learning environment of our universities is a part of the ethos that drives the Student Affairs profession, the value must translate into concrete activities. The initiative was successful in the sense that it attracted teaching faculty from across the campus who were interested in enhancing the learning environment. We named a space in our student union "The Learning Lounge." This space is frequently used for campus conversations and other learning activities. However, we were unable to construct a set of sustainable activities that could legitimately represent an initiative.

Subsequently, we have generated new initiatives in the areas of Statewide (Distant Student Services), Diversity, and Community Health to add to our continuing work on Assessment and Professional Development. The Transition initiative has been integrated into the Office of Admissions and Orientation and continues to use the same volunteer-driven leadership approach as the original effort.

Leadership and Learning

As mentioned earlier, our Compact was developed by a group of volunteers. From the beginning to the end of the process, we had approximately 150 people involved in the development of the core document. Including those who contributed to our Rights and Responsibility document, involvement surpassed 400 individuals. The processes associated with creating and leading the initiatives produced a dramatic transformation in our organizational culture.

It is important to understand the significance of the organizational climate at the time the Compact process was launched. It was a climate that fostered cynicism, isolation and fragmentation, mistrust, unkindness, and despair. The Compact served as a catalyst for the release of positive energy, renewed commitment to the organization, creation of new relationship networks, new leadership opportunities, the expression of creativity, and increased opportunities for learning.

The process used to develop the Compact and the learning that came through the process confirmed some of our beliefs about the potential of organizations and uncovered new learning in areas we had not anticipated. The learning related to grassroots leadership, the importance of relationships, and the benefits and liabilities of structure.

We learned that we are able to sustain focused dialogue with each other over an extended time period. This realization helped to create confidence that we have the capacity to struggle together and to produce the positive outcomes needed from us. This also served to disrupt the culture of disconnectedness and abandonment that people resorted to during times of challenge or duress. Beyond the positive relationships that occurred the purpose of our focused dialogue was to produce something of value to the university. The practice of being able to engage in and sustain difficult dialogue has become a central feature in our organizational style.

As we worked to develop the Compact, we learned that we could be productive in a nonhierarchical structure. To create a document such as the Compact and to construct the culture necessary to move it forward required that we function as a vision- and relationship-driven organization. We transformed ourselves from a leader-pushed to a vision-pulled organization. In the process, we learned to rely more on the power and energy that comes through our relationships and vision than on the power that comes through positional authority.

The leadership approach that was used to create the Compact was constructed on hope and faith. It assumed that there was a sufficient level of care and resiliency present in the organization and that people would be willing to take the risk to come forward, engage, and sustain engagement in the process. We learned that given space, opportunity, and an agenda people will step forward to lead and contribute. While the leadership approach modeled faith and hope, it is also important to acknowledge that the participants in the process brought their own faith and hope into the experience.

The positive outcomes produced by this effort bolstered members' expectations and created a foundation for members to have faith in our ability to produce positive change in other challenging situations.

A simple concept that we learned as we integrated the Boyer principles into our culture is that energy is the most important resource we have at our disposal. A fatigued organization has limited productivity. Though our organization has very intelligent, hard-working, and caring leaders, we achieved very little when we attempted to move the organization forward through the efforts of fatigued leaders. Although we were not able to do much to increase our financial resources, we were still able to achieve a tremendous amount through unleashing the personal, creative energy of colleagues throughout our organization.

Most important, this transformation revealed to us the significant role we need to play in modeling leadership, accountability, and responsibility to our colleagues across the campus. As we began the process and proclaimed our vision to be that "Student Affairs faculty and staff will provide leadership for the development of a positive sense of community at Oregon State University" (Division of Student Affairs, 1997), one participant asked, "Why will anybody follow us?" The response was, "Because nobody else is leading." Many in our organization were amazed at what we could achieve through seizing the leadership opportunities and filling the leadership void that existed at our university. It appeared that the question concerning whether others would honor Student Affairs as leaders grew out of a doubt about others' willingness to accept Student Affairs as a credible source of leadership. Through our work, we have proven to ourselves that not only are we seen as credible but we are honored and respected by others for our leadership.

Summary

Among our most meaningful achievements has been the establishment of positive, collaborative working relationships with our colleagues throughout the university. The Compact has led to the establishment of a culture of communication, collaboration, volunteerism, listening, and shared ownership that has significantly influenced Student Affairs and the rest of the campus. The Compact has also provided us with a guide to initiating relationships and constructing programs, initiatives, and activities, as well as to continuously redesigning our organization. As an outcome of our initiative process, we have created a culture in which it is customary for colleagues to span departmental boundaries to convene cross-functional groups to explore issues, develop programs, and solve shared problems. We have evolved to a place in our functioning where it is more the norm to collaborate than it is to work independently to advance organizational priorities.

The process of developing the Campus Compact has produced remarkable changes for the Division of Student Affairs at Oregon State University. The application of Boyer's principles has offered us a focal point around which to organize our efforts, build our relationships, and design our organization. Our members use the principles and the aspirations that we developed in relation to them as a source of accountability for those in our organization.

The story of Student Affairs at Oregon State University is not unlike the story of Student Affairs at many other institutions. The Compact process represented, for us, the means through which we reinvented ourselves. In each institution, there is a unique leadership form waiting to be claimed. Although institutions do share common elements, each must invent and create its own path. At Oregon State University, we have chosen to use the work of Ernest Boyer to construct our path to the future.

References

Boyer, E. L. (1990). *Campus life: In search of community*. Princeton, NJ: Princeton University Press.

Division of Student Affairs (1997). *The campus compact: A statement of vision, values and commitments*. Corvallis, OR: Oregon State University.

5

A Lab Without Walls

A Team Approach to Creating Community

Cathy Eidson Brown, J. Mark Brown,
and Robert A. Littleton

A decade ago, a group of Carson-Newman College administrators and faculty searched for a programming vehicle that would garner the interest and, ultimately, the financial backing of the "Strengthening Teaching and Learning in the First Two Years (STL)" initiative from the Pew Charitable Trusts. Given the structure of the grant, the Carson-Newman team was committed to the establishment of an educational experiment that would draw the long-term fiscal support of the institution's executive leadership. To survive beyond the Pew-Carnegie funding stage (one of the grant program's precepts), it was clear that it would have to be well received by several constituencies. Options were considered and dismissed, and the deadline grew ever closer. Bill McDonald, then dean of students for the institution, presented an idea born from his study of Ernest Boyer's philosophy that true learning should transcend classroom walls:

> During the first two years of college, Carson-Newman will instill in students an excitement for learning, sensitivity to culture and the arts, a curiosity about life, and the ability to think for themselves. . . . In a broad sense, students will understand their community responsibilities—to themselves, their traditions, other people, the environment, and the future. Students will get to know faculty

and staff personally, including how they live and what
motivates their life decisions [McDonald, personal communication, 1992].

Using Boyer's teaching as a compass point, the team reviewed
problems that could be addressed by the establishment of such a
program. Through a close-knit learning community of some 2,000
students and approximately 110 faculty members at the time, Carson-
Newman, like many schools of its size and heritage, struggled with
the problem of programmatic compartmentalization. Although
steeped in the best traditions of liberal arts education, the college
offered little in the way of incorporating its curricular components
seamlessly. Faculty members were mentoring juniors and seniors
well into their majors, but the college wanted nurturing relationships to be cultivated during the freshman and sophomore years. It
was likewise believed that providing a venue for faculty-student
connections earlier in the student's academic career would serve as
a retention tool.

How then, group members wondered, could a school of rather
static size and budget morph itself into a dynamic organism that
married the scholarship of classical learning with the sensory experience of practical application? As the grant would neither provide funds for capital investment nor sustain a new wave of faculty
mentors, McDonald and his colleagues set about envisioning a laboratory that enhanced learning. Suddenly, a proposal and a name
were born.

Boyer-Inspired Collaboration

In 1990, Boyer and The Carnegie Foundation for the Advancement
of Teaching recognized the urgency of addressing this problem. This
necessity for taking a fresh look at campus community led to the
challenge of developing visionary communities of learning in higher
education.

Similarly, Parker Palmer's essay, *Remembering the Heart of Higher Education* (1993), raised the issue by suggesting that institutions avoid a shortsighted quick fix for current problems. He argues, "We need a way of thinking about community in higher education that relates it to the central mission of the academy—the generation and transmission of knowledge" (p. 20).

Finally, the issue of a cocurricular education was also an important factor to the establishment of the Boyer Laboratory for Learning. Institutions needed to articulate the goals that an integrated cocurricular education would meet. Those who led the way in establishing Carson-Newman's Laboratory for Learning embraced the primary goal of a cocurricular education as the way to foster in students a vision for the connections between their experiences in and outside of class. Boyer (1987) notes, "Students must see the connection between what they learn and how they live, looking for the deeper significance, for the moral dilemmas and ethical responses" (p. 296) to the issues the students face on a day-to-day basis.

George Kuh and associates (1991) agree and encourage us to continue these efforts, noting:

> Because students spend more time out of class than in class, it would seem that learning could be enhanced if students were involved in such educationally purposeful out-of-class activities as institutional governance, leadership roles in student organizations, community service activities, and independent research projects. In fact, when asked about what they learned in college, graduates frequently mention that participation in outside activities increased their confidence, competence and self-assurance (Marchese, 1990). The research is unequivocal: students who are actively involved in both academic and out-of-class activities gain more from the college experience than those who are not so involved. [p. xi]

Customizing the Residential College Model

The issue of "working together" and the concept of "process" were important elements in Carson-Newman's attempt to customize a residential college model. Palmer (1981) preaches that higher education should "teach [all of us] to be supportive of and accountable to another; to deal creatively with competing interests; and understand [after all], that we are all in this together" (p. 79). Essentially, this was the attitude of the core group of faculty, administrators, and students who initiated the process to establish the Laboratory for Learning. The term *process* is a key factor in increasing community on campus. In *Laboratory for Learning: Promoting Community Learning Across Curricular and Co-curricular Functions*, Biddle, Lee, and McDonald (1998) comment on the process of community: "Community is desirable, but it cannot be declared. It is a process. And in our own efforts to build community on our campus, we initiated an ongoing project, which has taught us some essential components for building true community" (p. 70).

A core group of faculty, administrators, and students worked together to develop a proposal that would eventually lead to the Laboratory for Learning. The core group consisted of: a religion professor, an English professor, a biology professor, the assistant dean of academic affairs, the dean of students, a development officer, a resident director, an undergraduate student, and a graduate student. The core group's challenge was to develop not only a proposal that would qualify for the needed grant monies but be adaptable to Carson-Newman's campus.

The process for customizing a model for Carson-Newman was best described by Biddle and others (1998):

> A catalyst to spark community development is essential. In our case, the catalyst embarking on this project was an invitation to apply for a grant. While several of us

had been seeking ways to develop community, we lacked coordination and a specific goal. We had discovered a common conviction that while our institution described itself as a community, or a family, as though community were a *fait accompli,* we lacked an understanding that community constantly evolves. In short, the typical definition of community was grounded in a largely unexamined assumption that we—faculty, staff, students and administrators—all pursue a common purpose. Subsequently, a small group, emboldened by a shared sense of purpose and collegiality, coalesced and began to devise a new strategy for building a community on our campus [p. 71].

The result was a model similar to, yet different from, the traditional residential college model. The similarities were that both models focused on the residence halls as the primary place of implementing the cocurricular experience. And both models embraced the importance of student contact with faculty members. But the Laboratory for Learning differed from the traditional residential college in at least two ways. First, the Laboratory for Learning included administrators and staff, along with faculty members, in the working relationship with students. Second, with the Laboratory for Learning model, faculty members did not live in the residence hall they were serving, as would be the case with the traditional residential college model.

Fostering Community Through Co-Curricular Experiences

McDonald, Brown, and Littleton (1999) note the various ways cocurricular education exists on college campuses. These experiences are also what the Laboratory for Learning seeks to foster.

An integrated co-curricular education provides a variety
of opportunities for students to fully involve themselves
in their college education. Through residence hall life
and participating in student organizations, activities, and
campus ministries, students find themselves in living/
learning situations. Students learn to practice effective
communication with roommates, on the intramural field,
and during student governmental meetings. Students
often employ logical reasoning in late night debates in
the residence hall or by participating in team building
through a low ropes course. Through community service
and mission opportunities they learn personal and social
responsibility, gain world perspective, and experience a
continued deepening of civic service for the common
good [p. 37].

Along with the cocurricular experience for students, the issue
of stimulating faculty involvement was a primary focus as the program was in its beginning stages. Assigned the primary goal of developing a recruitment process to attract like-minded faculty to the
program, those who initiated the grant application worked together
to build a proposed participant list. Along with a stipend each semester, the faculty and administrators were allowed to use their residential fellow status to count as a college committee assignment,
which is expected of all faculty and staff.

Five faculty members and five administrators were identified to
serve on the five residential teams. All of the residential fellows participated in a weekend retreat that served as an orientation to the
program. From the program's inception, faculty and administrators
were able to interact with students in informal settings.

Admittedly, there was some apprehension about asking faculty,
staff, and administrators to participate for more than one semester.
To the surprise of the proposal team, the original group of faculty,
staff, and administrators who served on the first residential teams

asked for a commitment of three semesters. Their request was made because these individuals wanted to ensure continuity on their respective team. Overall, 95 percent of the original faculty, staff, and administrators completed their fifth semester of participation. This same level of commitment continued for the second generation, with 80 percent returning for a second year as residential fellows.

Goals for the Boyer Laboratory for Learning

The Laboratory for Learning has two distinct goals. First, the program seeks to expand the classroom to informal settings on campus. Although the residence halls are the driving force of the project, the program uses other campus settings and off-campus sites to involve a variety of campus constituents. Second, the program seeks to foster a stronger sense of community among faculty, staff, and students.

The original goal of the program was to establish seed communities that would produce a practical facsimile of the residential college. The concept of "Residential Teams" was implemented to foster utilization of these communities. In each of the college's five residence halls, a Residential Team consisting of a faculty member, administrator, the resident director, and three students was established and given the responsibility for planning and implementing programs designed to focus student attention on issues related to life and to academics.

It is important to note that the Boyer Laboratory for Learning has not superseded the work and responsibility of the Residence Life Department. The director of residence life, resident directors, resident assistants, and residence hall councils maintain a traditional residence life program. Social and educational programs and services are provided for residential students. However, the goals of the Residence Life Department and the Boyer Laboratory for Learning are similar and often provide opportunities for collaborative programming efforts.

The initial goal was to establish core teams within each residence hall that would seek to create broad and deep experiences for all students involved. In order to accomplish this, several things needed consideration. First, even though all residence halls had demographic and governmental similarities, there were subtle differences in the types of students residing in each building. For instance, the majority of male athletes resided in New Men's Hall, the largest residential facility on campus. Although the hall was the most modern residence hall at that time, it offered neither environmental advantages nor a sense of identity due to its size and structure. Teams assigned to the hall have focused on bringing students together with activities designed to initiate interaction with faculty and staff, as well as each other.

Second, the size, architecture, and culture of the residence halls were perceived as significant factors in shaping the diversity of programming. For example, Swann Hall, an elegant and stately building, is the oldest structure on campus. The "Victorian Christmas" celebration has become a time-honored tradition for the Swann residential team members. The event consists of decorating trees in each of the two main parlors during a period of caroling and enjoying food and fellowship. Although members of the campus community attend the event, the occasion has also established a sense of camaraderie among the residents of Swann Hall.

In order to consider the breadth and depth of experience the Laboratory for Learning yields, it is important to gain perspective from student participants. Carey Hall (Biddle, Lee, and McDonald, 1998) had these words to share concerning her experience:

> As Residential Fellows, we participate in planning with faculty and serve as liaisons between the students and faculty. Sometimes our events are a success—sometimes they're not. We learn through the process of planning what kinds of events students are most receptive to, how to bring students and faculty together, and just how much

this kind of situation often shocks a few people. The whole experience is what shapes the Lab for Learning program [p. 70].

Jennifer Elliott, another student residential fellow, also had some meaningful comments concerning her experience with the Laboratory for Learning.

Traditional roles and relationships are altered significantly when collaboration takes place. This approach to learning may positively influence the relationship of faculty and staff to students if the process is handled with proper respect by all participants. The students and traditional authority figures will eventually possess a more intense awareness of each other. In my experience, this promotes a higher level of accountability in the learning process while encouraging more playfulness and creativity, because the typical boundaries and roles are shifted and broken down [pp. 79–80].

Overall, the student residential fellow's continued familiarity with the distinctive features of their respective residence hall and connection with other students has proven to be an important contribution to the success of the program.

Creating Level Field to Stimulate Integrated Participation

Although Boyer's six principles of community create a noble philosophical framework for a theoretical community, it is no small task to accomplish such a feat. Community cannot be spoken into existence, nor can an oligarchy mandate that those people who live in close proximity to one another relate and interact in some transcendent fashion. Just as contemporary concepts of a subdivision and a neighborhood are mutually exclusive, so is the idea of a campus and a natural community.

In designing the Laboratory for Learning from Boyer's work, The Carson-Newman team unintentionally employed Benjamin Barber's concepts of "education as the training ground for democracy." Among seven points Barber makes in a sermonized chapter of *An Aristocracy of Everyone* (1992), published while the Carson-Newman proposal was in development, is his prescription that "empowerment [is] a necessary condition of the free community, for faculty and students" (p. 231). Granting that condition to an entire student body may well be desired to foster community; the implementation of it, however, is daunting to say the very least. The brilliance of the Boyer Lab's development was that its architects realized that it would require "seedling societies" in each residence hall to incubate the ideals of educational democracy.

As previously noted, the first hurdle was to ensure that students understood that not only was timidity unnecessary in the Boyer Lab, but it could be detrimental to the program's success. Like so many college students who are afraid of giving the wrong answer, those gathered for the program's first orientation retreat kept silent to the point of awkwardness. Finally, one young woman confided that she did not believe her participation would be of consequence. In the wake of her admission, others, including faculty and staff participants, confessed like concerns (Biddle, Lee, and McDonald, 1998).

Amy Gamble, director of Swann Hall and a residential fellow from 1998 to 2001, notes that even though the program has been in existence for eight years, new team members have to get used to the liberation found in the Boyer Laboratory.

> While traditional faculty/student roles tend to remain dominant in the initial stages of team formation, the team(s) I have been a part of realized that the building of relationships *is* the purpose of the Lab. When I was an undergraduate student, I don't recall being on a first

name basis with faculty or administrators. The Lab provides a unique opportunity that creates relationships that
transcend the norm. It's the best demonstration I have
seen of bringing real world experiences into the typical
college student's life [A. Gamble, personal communication, 2001].

Lab team members dispense with the use of academic and social
titles to nurture the sense of equality. Although it seems simple, not
having to call a faculty member Dr. or Professor or address an administrator as Mister, Mrs., or Miss is one of the first demonstrations
that a sense of equal status is possible. Teams are also encouraged not
to let particular tasks fall to those who may be perhaps more accustomed to them in the course of their day-to-day duties. An administrator might best know the operational point of budget process or how
to reserve a campus facility, but it is important that such responsibilities be spread out to provide confidence, ability, and ownership.

It is likewise important to the structural integrity of the team that
student members are offered and accept the equal footing granted by
the Boyer Lab experience. If the team is ever to be more than just
another campus programming committee, then nonmember residents of the building need to see first-hand the value of the group.
A residual benefit for faculty members is the opportunity to hone
their mentoring skills. As teaching methods adapt to contemporary
learning models, many professors are finding that traditional lecture
styles are often lost on eighteen- to twenty-four-year-olds raised on
MTV camera angles, cable modems, and microwave popcorn.

It is crucial to build each team's sense of community if there is
any hope of passing the ideals on to the building's residents who are
not part of the core group. Retreats and regular Boyer Lab meetings
are therefore vital to cultivating a communitarian ethic. It is likewise important that Boyer Fellows involve themselves in the life of
the particular hall they serve. A former member realized only after
he had rotated off a team that he had come to treat his service like

it was just another part of his job description. Although he says he enjoyed the two years he spent as a fellow, he admits that it was not as golden an experience as he thought it would be. "The problem was with me more than anything else," he recalls. "I often saw it as being just another meeting or one more event to note on the tally sheet. I would ultimately like to serve again because now I know what I would do differently."

Although it may appear utopian in concept, the residential fellows program is not easily managed because its objective is to eschew traditional hierarchical structures and work like a wheel built around the hub of common goals with fellows as the spokes; the wheel of the entire hall functions properly when balance and direction are maintained.

The Application of Boyer's Philosophy to Pauline Concepts of Equality

Carson-Newman's Christian mission has remained constant throughout its 150-year history. The vast majority of the student populations are practicing believers; in fact, 62 percent of the students identify themselves as being Baptist, which is the denominational heritage of the college. Most are familiar with the epistles of St. Paul and are especially so with his first letter to the Christians at Corinth. Many on campus believe that the theme of equality imbued in the Boyer Laboratory has a strong foundation in the apostle's writings.

> But God has combined the members of the body and has given greater honor to the parts that lacked it, so that there should be no division in the body, but that its parts should have equal concern for each other. If one part suffers, every part suffers with it; if one part is honored, every part rejoices with it. Now you are the body of Christ, and each one of you is a part of it [1 Corinthians 12: 24b–27 NIV].

Without a practical support, it would be lofty or demonstrative of a writer's hubris to claim a biblical foundation for a collegiate program. Like Barber, Boyer understood that education is key to establishing a truly functioning society.

Much like missionaries of democracy, residential fellows and the teams they make up serve the common good and mission of the Boyer Laboratory best when they celebrate their individualism while working in concert toward well-developed goals. Faculty and staff fellows who promote the legacy of the great educator's work are those who reach beyond the parameters of standard programming and avail themselves of student interaction.

One of the best appreciated of all Laboratory for Learning functions has been a traditional faculty sleep-over in New Men's Hall. Current students and recent graduates tell stories of playing basketball in the middle of the night with the vice president of student affairs and of taking favorite professors out to eat at the all-night restaurant by the interstate. A chemistry professor who is willing to sacrifice much-needed sleep and intestinal peace to share chili-cheese fries at 2 A.M. is surely the kind of person one can tell that one just can't remember the periodic table. And one would expect that the chemistry student who learned to talk to his professor about his own fears would become a friendly pharmacist, physician, or professor willing to listen to the concerns of a customer, patient, or student.

"Scholarship," argue Glassick and colleagues (Glassick, Huber, and Maeroff, 1997), has a moral aspect that should figure in all of its dimensions: discovery, teaching, integration and application" (p. 67). The goal of the Carson-Newman proposal team was that lab fellows would spend what amount to professional internships of interpersonal relationship building with the students they are helping prepare for the real world.

Central to building a solid team that can positively affect an entire hall is the understanding that members of each group function simultaneously as individual components and as part of a body. For a Christian institution such as Carson-Newman, there exists a heritage of faith that bolsters the concept.

"The body is a unit, though it is made up of many parts," wrote St. Paul, "and though all its parts are many, they form one body" (1 Corinthians 12:12 NIV). There is a distinct validity to an ideal espoused by the first century's greatest Christian missionary, Paul, that was redefined by a twentieth-century Quaker, Boyer, and effectively employed at a twenty-first-century Christian College, Carson-Newman.

Diamond in the Rough: Maintaining Dynamic Tension for Program Success

Bill McDonald admits that the original grant proposal seeking to create what became the Boyer Laboratory for Learning was license to consider a pipe dream. "Like most application projects, we sought to establish something that we would not and could not produce with existing funds," he recalls. "Being a small school with a limited endowment kept us from thinking about this sort of thing. So, once we started, to some degree, we shot the moon" (McDonald, personal communication, 2001).

To establish the philosophical mission from which the residential college experiment would be born, McDonald created the idea of a diamond. At the uppermost point of the diamond, he placed the program's mission. "Because we are committed to the idea that our programs utilize the overall mission of Carson-Newman, it only made sense to ensure that the Lab would fit into the college's philosophical scheme."

On one side of the diagram McDonald produced the idea of equality of voice. "We couldn't very well expect students to flourish if we did not clearly establish the right and duty to be an equal partner in the process." Shared ownership holds the vector to the other side of the paradigm. Ownership is the counterpart to equal voice because one cannot exist without the other, says the architect of the model. "By the time the first three elements were established, two things became quite clear. First, a program properly created on the outline of the diamond would create an intersection of creative tension. The second determination we made was the bottom point of the paradigm would be accountability" (W. McDonald, personal communication, 2001).

The Boyer Lab designers adopted the term *accountability* after initially using the word *autonomy*. Although the notion of individuals as autonomous creatures was most appealing, especially in light of its worth as a central Baptist doctrine, McDonald and company came to realize that autonomy, when put into practice, is often seen as the opposite of shared ownership. "There were potential ramifications that we thought might create fault lines in the practical application of the theory," he notes (W. McDonald, personal communication, 2001).

Although the four-pointed model immediately established the functional tension intended by its architects, McDonald says he has learned that too much focus on any of the four points ran the risk of sacrificing the functionality of the model. "When the model is working properly," he asserts, "there is a remarkable sense of freedom for each of the participants. In fact, my hope is that the model will endow in students the skills for responsible decision making that they can use for the rest of their lives. The unforeseen problem was that the tension is oftentimes an 'unbearable lightness of being' because the freedom is heavily dependent on proper use and in the correct proportion" (W. McDonald, personal communication, 2001).

Once established in concept and accepted for funding by the Pew Charitable Trust, the true test of the model's integrity came when the Laboratory for Learning was put into practice. The precepts designed in the vacuum of a grant proposal were put to a series of tests. Although many of the ideals served residential teams well, there were also many lessons to be learned.

The Lab for Learning in Practice: Organizational Schematic

In his book *Campus Life: In Search of Community*, Boyer (1990) writes that "by bringing together the separate parts, [colleges and universities can] create something greater than the sum, and offer the prospect that the channels of our common life will be renewed and deepened" (p. 63). These words capture the intent of the organizational schemata for the Laboratory for Learning. This section examines the Laboratory for Learning in practice and briefly explains the organizational schemata (see Exhibit 5.1).

Due to the nature of the grant, student participation on the residential teams was limited to sophomores. The aim of this initiative was to provide opportunities for students to connect with faculty, administrators, and staff early in their college experience. One central theme that was essential to the team process was that no one member would enjoy privilege or status, but all members would share equal responsibility for the team's development. Thus the concept of autonomy was to be a lesson studied with each new group. Since the program's inception, students have been particularly hesitant to express this freedom at first. However, with experience and support, the lesson becomes more manageable.

The overarching body for the Laboratory for Learning is the Steering Team. Although each team is autonomous, the Steering Team, identical in composition to residential teams, coordinates the work of the entire program. The Steering Team meets on a monthly basis. This time allows for lessons learned from past programs and future plans for various programming efforts. Every attempt is made to have all program-related decisions made (by consensus) at the team's monthly meetings. For example, throughout the life of the program, the Steering Team has decided to offer thematic programming across all teams. Such was the case during the 2000 Spring semester when the team chose "Sanctity of Human Life" as the theme for programming emphasis.

Team Profiles

In each of the five residence halls, a Residential Team was created, composed of residential fellows (now called Boyer Fellows), whose purpose was to create a cohesive and connected community, both among departments and among faculty, staff, and students. A desired outcome was for faculty, students, and staff on each residential team

Exhibit 5.1. Boyer Laboratory for Learning

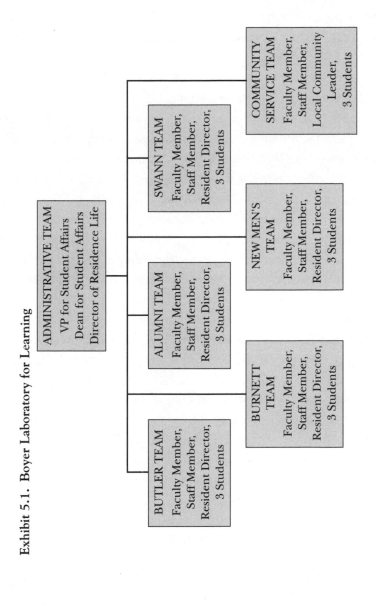

ADMINISTRATIVE TEAM
VP for Student Affairs
Dean for Student Affairs
Director of Residence Life

BUTLER TEAM
Faculty Member,
Staff Member,
Resident Director,
3 Students

BURNETT TEAM
Faculty Member,
Staff Member,
Resident Director,
3 Students

ALUMNI TEAM
Faculty Member,
Staff Member,
Resident Director,
3 Students

NEW MEN'S TEAM
Faculty Member,
Staff Member,
Resident Director,
3 Students

SWANN TEAM
Faculty Member,
Staff Member,
Resident Director,
3 Students

COMMUNITY SERVICE TEAM
Faculty Member,
Staff Member,
Local Community Leader,
3 Students

to share an excitement about learning and to know each other personally, including how each lived and was motivated. Residential teams consist of three students, a faculty member, an administrative staff member, and the resident director. Each student team member is expected to live in the residence hall of the team he or she is currently a member of.

Beginning in the 1999–2000 academic year, the program was expanded through a grant received from the Bonner Foundation to include a Community Service Team, which is composed of three students, a faculty member, an administrative staff member, and a local community member. In order to be more inclusive and seamless in their approach, the Boyer Leadership Team changed the title of residential fellows to Boyer Fellows. The inaugural community leader was a local civil rights activist who was instrumental in having Jefferson County recognize the Martin Luther King Jr. holiday. The Community Service Team focuses campus attention and resources on specific community service issues and initiatives. The student members of the Community Service Team may live in any residence hall or may live off-campus.

All participants maintain the title of Boyer Fellow after completion of their responsibilities. The Boyer Fellows wear honor cords at convocation, commencement, and all other official academic functions. Faculty and staff participants benefit by a reduction in committee assignments and by having their participation recognized and considered in tenure and promotion applications. All faculty, staff, and students receive a stipend each semester. Faculty, staff, and student participants may serve as a Boyer Fellow for two years before rotating off to allow new faculty, staff, and residents the opportunity to participate in the program. Resident directors serve every year to ensure the stability of the program.

Administrative Team Profile

An Administrative Team directs and coordinates the general operation of the Laboratory for Learning. The senior leadership of the Student Affairs Division represents the Administrative Team: the director of residence life, dean for student affairs, and the vice president for student affairs. The Administrative Team hires all faculty and staffs Boyer Fellows. Also, the team develops initial and ongoing training for all Boyer Fellows, administers the program's budget, and conducts program evaluations. Finally, the Administrative Team coordinates the selection of student Boyer Fellows through the six individual teams. Members of the Administrative Team serve every year to ensure the stability of the program.

Boyer's Endorsement and the Dedication of the Laboratory

Because Ernest Boyer's tenets of community had helped shape the formation of Carson-Newman's Laboratory for Learning, it was most fitting that he come to campus for the public unveiling of the program. Boyer enthusiastically shared his endorsement of the Laboratory for Learning in 1993, saying that he envisioned the development as an "enormously exciting innovation that will not only profoundly benefit the students of this campus, but also will serve as a model for the nation" (Biddle et. al., 1998, p. 74).

In March of 1997, after four years of steady growth, Carson-Newman renamed the program "The Ernest L. Boyer Laboratory for Learning" and dedicated it in the great educator's honor. His widow, Katherine Boyer, participated in the dedication ceremony where the campus community assembled and affirmed the Boyer Laboratory for Learning.

Boyer's life and writings continue to inspire the participants of the project that bears his name, as they seek to understand and create community in the unique residential college model he encouraged educators to pursue. Carson-Newman so esteems the program and the Boyer legacy that it presents its fellows with a white honor cord and grants them the right to wear it as part of their academic regalia. And whereas the Boyer legacy has brought the institution much local media attention and national acclaim, including the National Association of Student Personnel Administrators' (NASPA's)

Innovative Programs award and a citation by the Templeton Foundation as a Character Building Program, it nonetheless remains first and foremost a cocurricular education instrument designed to extend teaching beyond classroom walls.

The Pragmatic Application

When teams were initially established in each of the five residence halls, the immediate objective of each group was to plan events and provide programs that would create for the resident population the idea that the Laboratory for Learning offered unique experiences that happened to be educational. The objective behind the strategy was to provide value-added interaction that would pave the way for incorporating the tailor-made residential college model.

In the program's first year, all three female Laboratory for Learning teams planned a women's conference that was an immediate and huge success. The hall fellows worked as a team, with each member taking his or her assigned task and seeing it to fruition. Initially unsure of the response they would garner, team members were pleasantly shocked when some sixty women registered for the event. Participant evaluations confirmed the worth of the event, and it was decided it would be offered again.

A year later, the team followed the conference plan they had used the first time, expecting similar results. Sadly, the second offering was a bust. "I think we are too ready and willing to try and make a successful event a tradition," says one of the administrative directors of the Lab. "It's as if we think it will always work because it worked well one time. It's a lesson some of our teams have had to learn more than once."

Although certain programs proved successful and became traditions over the course of several years, including Swann Hall's "Victorian Christmas," many of the best programs were one-time offerings that are remembered by participating students as watershed college experiences. An otherwise routine hiking and camping trip became a gilded memory when the outing ended at the grave of the man for whom Jeff Daniel Marion wrote *Fishing at Emmert's Cove*. As Carson-Newman's distinguished poet-in-residence, Marion was a campus legend who was willing to read and discuss his work in the setting in the very place where the muse came to him. The novelty of such an event, coupled with the access to a regionally famous author, drew an awed response from those on the sojourn. In the wake of the "Saving Private Ryan" phenomenon, this Boyer Laboratory event focused on the Normandy recollections of an area pastor who had stormed Utah Beach on D-Day. As he carried his listeners from skirmishes to battles across Western Europe that evening, recalling whizzing bullets and failed mortar blasts, those in attendance came to understand the supernatural power that compelled him to spend his life as a minister. Although the film created the demand for the event, it was the quality of the program that gave the student fellows credibility with the residents.

"The program is one of the most unique opportunities I've ever been a part of in an educational setting," noted student fellow Carey Hall, when asked to chart her personal growth through the Boyer Lab. "Besides learning to bond with professors on a hike or in a tent in the middle of a lethal rainstorm, we've learned to enjoy reading Thoreau in the midst of a cool autumn night." It is most interesting that the structure of Hall's assessment of the Lab followed the objectives set into motion by McDonald and his fellow architects. "Besides sharpening our planning skills," continued Hall, "we've learned how to work effectively with a diverse team that included different insights, educational levels and degrees of stamina. On top of all this, we've learned that education often happens when we open our minds to new people, new ideas and new opportunities. We learn the goodness of things unseen and educate ourselves in a sphere of creativity" (Biddle et. al., 1998, p. 74).

Teams have periodically joined together to cosponsor major events such as concerts, lectures, and Welcome Week festivities intended to market the Boyer Laboratory for Learning campuswide.

And although the branding of the Boyer Lab has finally begun to take root in the mind of students, it has not necessarily followed the stellar trajectory intended by its designers. Eight years after its founding, Carson-Newman administrators charged with directing the Boyer Laboratory for Learning say that even though the program has been an overall success, they admit they first began to develop concerns as the Lab grew beyond its infancy. At its best, they say, the Lab has mirrored the traditional residential college model, save the fiscal encumbrances of added salaries and special facilities. However, problems have arisen when specific residential teams have slipped into the default mode of serving as programming committees.

"I think it is analogous to the creative tension suggested by the diamond model," says McDonald. "When teams offer the right blend of programming and faculty/staff interaction, cocurricular education experiences blossoms. When there is more interaction than programming, it amounts to just hanging out with professors, and when programming becomes the absolute focus, it just becomes another campus event" (W. McDonald, personal communication, 2001).

The Carson-Newman vice president of student affairs says the Boyer Laboratory is now rooted deeply enough that it can undergo certain changes to grant it a new focus. His plan includes releasing the Lab from its five separate residential fellow teams and creating a campus team with a broader focus.

The Impact of the Boyer Lab

As part of the overall residence life evaluation, students are given the opportunity to give feedback on programs and services provided by the Residence Life Department. In January 2000, all residential students (1,011 students) received a copy of the "Residence Life Satisfaction Survey." A portion of the survey was directed toward the Boyer Laboratory for Learning. Students had the option of not filling out the survey, filling out the survey and mailing it to the Campus Life Office, or filling out the survey and returning it to their resident assistant. The overall return rate for the survey was 68 percent. Results were entered into the computer program Microsoft Excel. An assistant professor of mathematics then compiled and analyzed the results. A brief synopsis of the results pertaining to the Boyer Laboratory for Learning is discussed in this section.

Based on a 5-point Likert Scale, the average scores (shown in parentheses) for all respondents were as follows:

I am familiar with the Laboratory for Learning. (3.41)

I am familiar with the purpose of the Laboratory for Learning. (3.15)

The Laboratory for Learning has had a positive impact on my experience at Carson-Newman. (3.14)

Overall, we discovered that at least 41.7 percent of respondents had attended at least one Laboratory for Learning event while at Carson-Newman. Similarly, 49.7 percent of survey respondents indicated that the Laboratory for Learning provided programs that addressed issues appropriate to their residence hall.

One of the survey questions was aimed at measuring the familiarity of the purpose of the Boyer Laboratory for Learning. Using the chi-square method of analysis (chi-square = 25.893, DF = 12, Pvalue = 0.011), a strong association is indicated between familiarity with the purpose of the Laboratory for Learning and the individual residence halls. The percentage of residents who agree that they are familiar with the purpose of the Laboratory for Learning varies from hall to hall. Residents from the two smallest residence halls are more likely to be familiar with the purpose; residents from the largest hall are less familiar with the purpose.

There was also a significant finding in terms of familiarity with the purpose of the Laboratory for Learning and classification. Using chi-square analysis (chi-square = 40.868, DF = 9, Pvalue= 0.00), a strong association was shown between familiarity with the Laboratory for

Learning and classification. The higher the class, the more familiar the students are with the purpose of the Laboratory for Learning. Seniors are more familiar with the purpose than freshmen. Approximately 53 percent of seniors indicated they had attended at least one Laboratory for Learning event, as compared to 37 percent of freshmen. Similarly, 60 percent of the seniors thought the Laboratory for Learning provided programs that addressed issues appropriate to their residence hall, as compared to 39 percent of freshmen.

The association between overall residence hall satisfaction and positive impact from the Laboratory for Learning should also be mentioned. Chi-square analysis (chi-square = 26.246, DF = 6, Pvalue = 0.00) reveals a strong association between satisfaction and positive impact from the Laboratory for Learning. Residents who agree that they have been positively affected by the Laboratory for Learning are more likely to be satisfied with their experience in the residence halls at Carson-Newman.

These findings, as well as others that resulted from the survey and other evaluation measures, are useful as we continue the Laboratory for Learning. We believe that all students in all residence halls can be affected in some way through the Laboratory for Learning. Inevitably, some will be affected more than others, as is true for seniors who are more familiar with the program's purpose than freshmen. The same could be said of other campus programs, as upperclassmen are often more connected with the institution due to their years of experience. Although the small residence halls indicated a greater likelihood of being familiar with the purpose of the Laboratory for Learning, all sizes of residence halls can and do benefit from such a program.

Over the course of the Boyer Lab's existence, residential fellows have been constantly solicited for their input on the program and its effectiveness. Although there have been certain negative responses to individual programs offered through the particular teams, the feedback cultivated about the Boyer Lab itself has been overwhelmingly positive.

"Often times I do not enjoy committee work, and really do not look forward to it," a faculty member wrote. "However, with this project I feel a sense of honor being associated with our work." Although the response is decidedly positive, it is revealing in that the Lab fellow still saw her participation at some level as the committee duties expected as part of her contract.

The response of another faculty member demonstrates the transforming quality that was intended in the experiment from its hypothesis. "I get really excited about an idea like this and its ability to transform the campus and make a difference in people's lives," he wrote at the end of his first year. "It reminds me of a Beatles' song, 'There's going to be a revolution.'"

There is inherent in many of the responses a certain innocence and novelty to getting to know faculty members. A resident of Alumni Residence Hall submitted his evaluation of a midnight breakfast with faculty members at an area restaurant. He wrote, "I learned that some of the faculty can be cool and just chill. This was a sweet experience!" He further admitted that he learned something most professors at small private schools wish their students understood. "Teachers are really nice and concerned about students' lives." He continued, "I met two new faculty members I didn't know—keep up the good work!"

A non-Boyer faculty member matched his young counterpart's assessment: "I got acquainted with several students I would not have otherwise met. . . . I wouldn't change a thing." One can assume that Ernest Boyer himself would have been pleased to see the gelling of community over a late-night meal at an all-night eatery. "I had a rare opportunity to spend time with a number of young men," he noted. "I got to find out about their backgrounds and interests and get an impression of the mind-set and spirit of current students."

Catherine Graham, a former Carson-Newman faculty member who was on one of the first-generation teams, perhaps summed up the experience best (C. Graham, personal communication, 1994): "I think I have become a better teacher and colleague through my experience with this special program. I will strive to encourage my students to participate in learning beyond their classroom experiences, and I continue to learn how to make learning more interesting and more relevant to the students' daily lives."

Nicole Climie, who served as a student fellow, wanted to ensure that her replacement understood the value of the Lab (N. Climie, personal communication, 1994). "Whoever you are who is going to take my position," she wrote, "let me encourage you to put your efforts and enthusiasm into this. It is a cause well worth your time and if no one else benefits, you certainly will. I did—I got to know [people] who otherwise would have just been faces to me."

Carson-Newman's Ernest L. Boyer Laboratory for Learning is—like all communities worth being a part of—dynamic, in flux, mixed with progress and regression, blessed by diverse backgrounds and personalities, plagued by deadlines and mundane tasks, and after several generations alive and vibrant. Gerald Wood, chair of the English Department, found that the "Boyer Lab for Learning is the best way for faculty and students to remind ourselves that education—in the best sense—is never limited by time and place. No matter on which side of the lectern we find ourselves, the Lab helps us bring excitement, growth, and wonder into the college experience" (G. Wood, personal communication, 2001).

References

Barber, B. (1992). *An aristocracy of everyone*. New York: Oxford University Press.

Biddle, M. E., Lee, E. D., & McDonald, W. M. (1998). *Laboratory for learning: Promoting community learning across curricular and co-curricular functions*. In R. R. Jenkins & K. T. Romer (Eds.), *Who teaches? Who learns? Authentic student/faculty partners* (pp. 67–80). Providence, RI: Ivy Publishers.

Boyer, E. L. (1990). *Campus life: In search of community*. Princeton, NJ: Princeton University Press.

Boyer, E. L. (1987). *College: The undergraduate experience in America*. New York: Harper & Row.

Glassick, C. E., Huber, M. T., and Maeroff, G. I. (1997). *Scholarship assessed: Evaluation of the professoriate* (Special Report: Carnegie Foundation for the Advancement of Teaching). San Francisco: Jossey-Bass.

Kuh, G. D., Schuh, J. H., Whitt, E. L., & Associates (1991). *Involving colleges: Successful approaches to fostering student learning and development outside the classroom*. San Francisco: Jossey-Bass.

Marchese, T. J. (1990). A new conversation about undergraduate teaching: An interview with Professor Richard J. Light, convener of the Harvard Assessment Seminars. *AAHE Bulletin, 42*(9), 3–8.

McDonald, W. M., Brown, C. E., & Littleton, R. A. (1999). The Ernest L. Boyer laboratory for learning: A model of effective faculty involvement in residential programming. *College Student Affairs Journal, 19*(1), 35–43.

Palmer, P. J. (1981). *The company of strangers: Christians and the renewal of America's public life*. New York: Crossroad.

Palmer, P. J. (1993). Remembering the heart of higher education. AAHE's 1993 National Conference on Higher Education. Washington, DC: American Association of Higher Education.

6

Promoting Community Through Citizenship and Service

Jean L. Bacon

In order to share our vision in imparting the value of citizenship and service to students, we must build programs that include university-community collaboration. These collaborative efforts can be used to address the growing requirements of society. Institutions of higher education, as members of the community, are challenged not just to educate and create knowledge but to engage the community through service and civic responsibility. This commitment to the well-being of the community enriches and enhances a diverse society.

At institutions of higher education, students have the opportunity to explore diverse relationships, gain leadership skills, develop critical thinking, and search for the ways in which they can contribute to society, leaving it different and better than they found it. This chapter discusses one example of a student affairs specialization that prepares graduate students to employ citizenship and service in the creation and maintenance of community collaborations. This specialization exemplifies the promotion of citizenship and service in encouraging leadership development.

In order to fully understand the necessity for the student-community development specialization, one must have some knowledge of The State University of New York (SUNY) at Stony Brook.

Introduction to SUNY at Stony Brook

"To Learn—To Search—To Serve" is SUNY's motto, underscoring the value this institution places on the search for knowledge, on teaching, and on service. SUNY at Stony Brook is one of the sixty-four campuses that make up the public university system of the state of New York. Stony Brook is a research university that confers degrees ranging from undergraduate to doctoral degrees.

SUNY at Stony Brook is located on a 1,100-acre campus on Long Island's affluent north shore. The university has a budget of $800 million, with enrollment of 20,000 students. The majority of undergraduate students are from New York; 58 percent of graduates are international students. Sixty percent of the student body is Caucasian, as is 83 percent of the faculty. The university employs 12,000 people and is the largest single-site employer in the area.

The School of Social Welfare, where the student-community development specialization is offered, has approximately 67 undergraduates, 308 graduate, and 30 doctoral students. The school was opened in 1971 to address social injustices in society. The School of Social Welfare offers a master's degree in social welfare, the purpose of which is to provide education and practicum experience in the field of social work. Students obtain generalist knowledge and skills in the areas of health, policy, and social work practice and how they affect individuals, families, groups, communities, and organizations. The school's mission is entrenched in the belief that all individuals, regardless of culture, ethnicity, disability, gender, socioeconomic status, and sexual preference, have a right to a quality existence free from discrimination and oppression. All students in the School of Social Welfare must perform planned and structured community service with a commitment to serve the underserved and the traditionally disadvantaged. Students are involved in civic matters and have leadership responsibilities on the campus and in the larger community.

Student Affairs and Social Welfare

The specialization came about as a result of an initiative by the vice president of student affairs to develop a curriculum that would challenge the university to respond to Boyer's legacy in building and maintaining an inclusive and engaged learning community. The core of this innovative specialization is to teach and motivate students to renew the focus of quality in campus and student life. The specialization was born out of an attempt to partner student affairs and social welfare to address the changing needs of the contemporary college landscape. The goal was to create a program that prepared student affairs professionals to build and maintain community on university campuses and beyond the walls of the traditional campus purview.

In the negotiations with a professional school to collaborate with both the Office of the Vice President of Student Affairs and the School of Social Welfare, the proposal for a student-community development specialization was deemed well suited for both disciplines. In response to the changing needs of the contemporary college landscape, a group of administrators, staff, and faculty at the university met to discuss ways in which these changes might be addressed. The decision was made that a nontraditional student affairs personnel program was needed to prepare administrators who would be cognizant of providing an atmosphere for students in which learning and professional development occurs in enlightened ways.

From its inception, the student-community development specialization was intended as a way to use social change models to correct social injustices that affect college and university campuses and extended communities. Much thought and strategic planning was invested in the choice to place this specialization in the School of Social Welfare.

The specialization was designed to address the lapses in traditional student affairs personnel programs. Among the most salient lapses were in training student affairs administrators to promote leadership, speak to multicultural campus issues, and emphasize the role of colleges and universities as citizens. The reasons for supporting the specialization's placement in the School of Social Welfare included

- The field practicum requirement

- The importance of social change to the knowledge base

- The presence of established community collaborative relationships

This nontraditional program has built a complementary relationship between student personnel administration and social welfare, melding the ethics and values of both disciplines to build a solid foundation for training student community educators. In the specialization, students are encouraged to build community by taking on leadership roles and responsibilities for both the campus and extended community of which they are an integral part. Citizenship and service are honored by being at the core of both the university's and the school's mission and is well integrated into the creation of a student affairs education program. The specialization demonstrates an understanding that it is not enough for institutions of higher education to create and dispense knowledge from the ivory tower. Colleges and universities must form collaborative relationships in which all parties create, contribute, and plan in ways that benefit the good of all society, not just an elite few. Student affairs administrators who are trained from this model will go on to bring diverse people together to combat social injustices and to affect social need while building knowledge.

The challenges of creating a collaborative specialization presented themselves in

- Finding faculty who could teach both social welfare and the student affairs curriculum

- Providing students with experiential learning in higher education administration

- Blending the two disciplines to create a sound curriculum

Student Community Development Specialization

The components of this novel program include classroom, service, and experiential learning accompanied by opportunities for leadership. Students are required to take classes in theory, practice, and contemporary issues in higher education. Students must also intern in a field environment to gain hands-on knowledge of the role of a community educator, as well as the expectation placed on them to hold positions of campus leadership. This chapter examines the curriculum rationale and future goals of the student-community development specialization.

The specialization offers a unique professional partnership between social welfare and student affairs–student personnel in higher education. The specialization permits social welfare students at the master's level to obtain knowledge of social work practice as it pertains to the contemporary college campus. Students develop skills in addressing a range of issues that affect the diverse population of university students. Experience and intervention skills are developed in providing direct interventions in response to the campus life concerns, such as maintaining and building community, interracial and intercultural relations, safety, civility, and substance abuse. The campus concerns that students research are current with the needs of the contemporary college campus. Specialization students are taught to understand the impact that variables such as gender, ethnicity, culture, and socioeconomics have on student wellness and influence a student's sense of belonging and commitment to the larger campus community. The ways in which college personnel can encourage the process of inclusiveness versus exclusivity are explored with emphasis on nurturing community wellness.

The student-community development specialization places an emphasis on organizational and community development, social change, and the strengths and empowerment perspectives as vital components of social work practice within institutions of higher education. This ingenious graduate program called Student-Community Development is a two-year program of study leading to a master's degree in social welfare with a specialization in student-community development.

Social welfare students are prepared for administrative positions in student personnel arenas in institutions of higher education. Teaching modalities include collaboration and experiential learning. The ethics and values of social welfare and student personnel services guide the training and mission of this specialization.

The belief that underscores the premise of the specialization is that the campus community includes the extended community locally, nationally, and internationally. Institutions of higher education have a responsibility to teach and thoroughly communicate the values of citizenship and service; these values embody the purpose and future goals of the specialization. Incorporated in the mission of the student-community development specialization is the doctrine that, as part of their academic learning, students must feel a spirit of mutual accountability for building community and affecting social change (Bacon, 2000).

Curriculum

"The integration of the disciplines of social work and student personnel education guide the curriculum to focus on: community organization, social justices, cultural diversity, student development theory, wellness models and institutional change" (McDonald and others, 2000, p. 12). Students are mandated to follow the school's curriculum and take the additional specialization course work, fulfilling requirements of both.

The specialization focuses on theory, as well as on developing practical skills in the development, implementation, management, and evaluation of social, health, and educational policies and programs. Students trained in the specialization learn to be community development educators working in a wide range of roles as administrators, managers, program and policy analysts, program coordinators, planners, advocates, and community organizers.

Course emphasis is on the following contemporary content areas relevant to practice within educational settings: multiculturally competent practice, assessment, crisis intervention, substance abuse intervention, student development theory, community-based advocacy, legal issues and risk management, and higher education administrative systems.

The curriculum that students in the specialization complete allows them to become familiar with student affairs and the structure of institutions of higher education. Students must understand the varied roles of a student affairs administrator as well as the knowledge base that supports this role. A wide range of skills that are relevant to successful practice in the arena of higher education are taught. The curriculum for students in the specialization is as follows:

Student-Community Development Core

Student-Community Development Colloquia I & II

Student-Community Development Seminar I & II & III

Student-Community Development Issues in Higher Education

Contemporary Issues in Higher Education

Master's Project Team Thesis

Field Practicum

Leadership Symposium

Required Foundation Courses

Field Instruction I–IV (III and IV in Higher Education setting)

Human Behavior and the Social Environment I and II

Social Work and Health

Advanced Social Work Micro Practice I and II

Advanced Social Work Macro Practice I and II

Social Work Research I and II

Parameters of Social and Health Policy I and II

Social Work Practice I and II (Bacon and others, 2000)

Students must complete course work sequentially with their co-hort, which leads to the building of cohesive student groups. The specialization accepts a maximum of fifteen students a year, providing a climate for building student-to-student and student-to-faculty relationships. Students form a network of support, which improves individual and group problem solving and critical thinking, as well as interpersonal relationship skills. All courses are co-taught by both an individual with a master's in social work and one employed in student affairs or student personnel administration. By receiving instruction from a professor of social welfare and a student affairs administrator, students benefit from the professional expertise, knowledge base, and experiential examples of both disciplines. Co-taught classes rely on modeling collaboration and illustrating interdisciplinary partnerships. Classes are also taught by visiting lecturers who have special expertise in a featured area.

The course work that is offered introduces the student-community development model as an integrated application of social work, community organizations and student development theories, and practice modalities. Courses examine the history of higher education as it relates to the evolution of the American college campus and changes in student culture and needs. As a result, students become familiar with the inception of both disciplines.

The courses are designed to be consistent with the school's mission, which emphasizes the values of human dignity and of social and economic justice. The courses emphasize a strength and empowerment perspective and are intended to examine how political, socioeconomic, cultural, and health issues affect higher education. This perspective identifies and respects the intrinsic worth of all persons, their construction of reality, and the diversity of their experiences and cultures.

The first semester provides an overview of historical literature, including: student development theory, higher education administration, and student demographics. Connections are made between social work practice theories, health issues, and field practicum concerns. The semester concludes by connecting major contemporary campus issues to the role of the social worker affecting social change.

The second semester builds on the foundation of knowledge and skills developed in the first part of the course. Students are introduced to the concept of campus community as it relates to systems theory. Specific social change strategies and intervention skills are introduced and developed by students in the final sessions of the course. Course content also focuses on providing students with an understanding of community building on contemporary campuses of higher education and the role of social workers in that setting as they attempt to ameliorate issues of student concern.

These courses provide an introduction to the professional outcome of community development educators. Part of the course requirement is that students participate in planning, implementing, and evaluating the Annual Student-Community Wellness Leadership Symposium, which is a major event sponsored by the specialization. Upon completion of the colloquia, first-year generalist course work, and field practicum, students are prepared to fulfill the second-year requirements of a field practicum in higher education arenas.

Student-community development seminars are three-semester seminars that examine how political, socioeconomic, cultural, and health issues affect higher education. Drawing on strengths and empowerment perspectives, the seminar emphasizes how the variables just described influence and shape student community wellness on the college campus. Students in the seminar critically examine contemporary higher education structures, planning modalities, and intervention strategies for accomplishing the goals set by institutions of higher education.

Using campus-based studies, students explore and develop intervention strategies, organizational structures, and planning parameters that will facilitate the process of bringing social change to institutions of higher education. The role of the community educator in higher education and the role students will play as future change agents are also examined. Students and faculty explore concerns that face individuals and groups as they attempt to negotiate the college environment.

Through the use of the case method model of learning, students are presented with material that presents the dilemmas of university administrators and student affairs personnel as they strive to foster and promote a sense of campus community. Students are encouraged to consider the ways in which social workers can advance community development on college campuses. Students discover the prevalence, history, and impact these current issues exert in higher education, using the methods of conflict management, resolution, and mediation as a framework for advancing positive change.

Specific social change strategies and intervention skills are introduced and developed by students. Major contemporary campus issues are connected to the role of social workers in working toward social change. The course focuses on providing students with an understanding of community building on contemporary campuses and the role of social workers in that setting who are working toward social change as they attempt to ameliorate issues of student concern and conflict.

Field Practicum

Specialization founders were concerned about arranging experiential learning opportunities in local colleges and universities. Institutions of higher education were accustomed to the traditional social work students and their role in counseling centers, but they did not understand the new role. It required much networking and meeting to present the student affairs social worker to the professional realm of student affairs administrators. The School of Social Welfare requires on-site social work supervision for student interns; in student affairs it was rare to find a social worker to provide supervision. This problem was resolved by hiring a social work supervisor specifically for students in the specialization.

The first year of field instruction for specialization students is completed in a "traditional" social work placement arena; the second-year's work occurs at an institution of higher education. The field practicum site is any college or university in an office or department under student affairs. Second-year internships are served in the "offices of student affairs, deans of students, international student affairs, career placement, student services and disabled students services among others. As part of the internship experience students conduct and analyze research, complete administrative tasks, write grants, have committee memberships, design and implement student and faculty programs and have student contact. The students have leadership roles on campus and are visible in their commitment to building campus community as it pertains to the greater campus and its extended communities" (McDonald and others, 2000, p. 12).

Examples of field placement include assignment as a program coordinator at New York University in the LGBT (lesbian, gay, bisexual, and transgender) Student Center. In this placement, the student designed and implemented programs, provided advisement, and advocated for LGBT students as they negotiated the campus community. An international student was placed in the International Students Office, where one of her tasks was to conduct a needs assessment of international student and service delivery at SUNY at Stony Brook.

Leadership Symposium

Every year the student-community development specialization sponsors a leadership symposium. Two presidents from institutions of higher education and one administrative leader are invited to speak to the staff, faculty, and students on a contemporary issue that is pertinent to campus communities. The past symposium topics have included multiculturalism, the engaged university community, the international student, and violence in education. Administrators, staff, faculty, and community leaders are invited to attend. First-year specialization students' tasks for the day's events include: hosting the morning session, introducing the invited speakers to the campus community, and planning programs. As a result of the symposium, students learn event and program planning and working in a committee, along with specific information about the topic presented. This event presents the students with an opportunity to speak one-on-one with university officials and gives them a chance to debate and discuss issues that have a major impact on campus community and student well-being.

The International Component

The specialization, for the first time in the Spring and Summer semesters 1999–2000, added an international component to the opportunities offered to students. Two students were chosen via interview and written essay to travel to sites where they could experience an international exchange. Students spent the spring semester at Our Lady of the Lake University and the University of the Incarnate Word in San Antonio, Texas, completing academic course work, preparing for teaching English to Chinese students, and serving internships. The summer for the first year of students who participated was spent in China, where they learned about the culture of the country's education system, role of teachers, building international relationships, and understanding diverse international populations. Providing service on an international level exposed students to global social needs and forced them to examine issues outside the United States. This experience led to personal and professional development for both students. They learned about a culture unlike their own and witnessed a different way of life. The students struggled with being separated from their families and the material and emotional comforts of home. On their return, students

presented a symposium to the entire campus community of their experiences and were recently noted in the National Association of
Student Personnel Administrator's *Focus*.

Assistantships

A number of half-time (ten hours per week) graduate assistantships
are granted in the Office of the Vice President for Student Affairs
to first-year students. The primary tasks of these assistantships are
to assist with student affairs research that is currently being conducted, including measurement construction, data analysis, and the
preparation of written reports.

The time commitment is ten hours per week from the end of
August through the beginning of June and is in addition to field
placement. As compensation, students receive a full tuition waiver
and a stipend (amount determined by the graduate students' union
contract) for the academic year of the assistantship. In order to ensure that the assistantships are awarded in an equitable and fair
manner, each interested student is required to submit a letter of
interest and a resumé and then to be interviewed. The criteria for
selection include prior research experience or knowledge, communication and time-management skills, computer literacy, and overall enthusiasm.

There are a number of graduate assistantships available on the
university campus that give the student experience in the campus
environment. Currently, only the assistantships in the Office of the
Vice President for Student Affairs are exclusively held and granted
to first-year students. However, many areas around the campus are
interested in hiring students enrolled in the specialization.

Fellowships

The Reginald C. Wells Multicultural Affairs Fellowship and the
Reginald C. Wells Commuter Student Services Fellowship are
granted to two second-year students on a competitive basis. The
time commitment is twenty hours per week from the end of August

through the beginning of June (in addition to field placement). Students who are chosen are permitted to complete their field practicum for their second year in the Master's of Social Welfare Program at the site of their fellowship. The fellowship tasks and hours must be differentiated from the field practicum work assignments and hours. As compensation, students receive a full tuition waiver and a stipend. "Second-year students are eligible to apply for the fellowships with the office of the Dean of Students for the Commuter Student and for the Multicultural Affairs Fellowship. The fellows work closely with the Dean to design and implements programs in Commuter Students and Multicultural Affairs Offices" (McDonald and others, 2000, p. 13).

"The specialization also has two Americorps fellows working in the community to provide computer-learning opportunities for children and families in socio-economically distressed communities" (McDonald and others, 2000, p. 13). Two SUNY Stony Brook students who were chosen to be Americorps Fellows collaborated with a local community to create a family learning center. The Americorps Fellows negotiated with local businesses and organizations and met with the school board to supply thirty computers to a local elementary school. The fellows conducted technology training and education to families in a low-socioeconomic community. Students coordinate the staff and faculty of the center, as well as the community members, to address the technology divide that remains between those with access and knowledge of computers and those without. Through the engagement of student leaders and the commitment of community members and the university, a social need is being addressed.

The Americorps Fellows spoke in depth of their relationships with students at the local school where they performed their fellowships:

> We could not envision the amount of work it would take
> to get the Center up and running. We had to rely on
> ourselves, if tasks were not completed things did not run

smoothly and the responsibilities were all on us. I did not believe that the students would miss us when we left. The students have given us such a hard time as we tried to teach them. At the end of the fellowship we realized the impact of our presence and hard work. The students let us know in their own way that we would be missed.

The fellows' statements give insight into the power of mentoring and teaching relationships. In the beginning of the assignment, the students were unsure of the task that lay ahead; after the assignment was completed, they marveled at all they had accomplished. The learning that occurred is immeasurable. In this instance, the collaborative relationship between so many local organizations, the school district, businesses, and SUNY at Stony Brook made a great difference. This venture paved the way for more campus-community collaborations.

Basic Premise

Students learn to use an integrative community development model created by Stein, Preston, Goldstein, and Segall (1997). The basic premises supporting this theoretical model of the specialization are as follows:

- Colleges and universities must promote social change that nurtures a strong community.

- Social change, in the context of democratic ideals, citizenship, and social justice, is enhanced through shared leadership, which celebrates both individuality and collaboration.

- Optimal community development is grounded in a strategic set of democratic values.

- Community development is a process of shared responsibility that nurtures individual and group empowerment.

- Individual and community growth and responsibility are interdependently linked.

- Individuals and groups have physical, emotional, and cognitive competencies.

- Education is a lifelong experiential and cognitive learning process.

- Maximally effective learning environments are participatory and interactive.

- The learning community extends beyond the physical boundaries of the classroom and campus.

Opportunities for Leadership

The university's mandate focuses on Boyer's principles of an engaged campus community, which supports the provision of opportunities for students. We are all encouraged to understand that effectiveness in a learning imperative can only occur if we build relationships with the larger extended community. In this vein, students must understand the value in service contributions. We are all responsible to each other; we are our brother's keeper, connected by our humanity. The value of service, volunteerism, and citizenship is that we come to have a knowing of our purpose and meaning in this society. We come to understand our place here on earth. "Acknowledging our responsibility to contribute to the wider fellowship of life" (Bellah and others, 1996, p. x), the rhythm and pattern of our lives have become intertwined in contributing to the well-being of others who may or may not look like us, who may or may not speak the same language as us, but who share in the human struggle of attempting to live a good life. Social obligation of the institution to contribute practically to the extended community is supported by the specialization.

Specialization students must contribute to the public good via internships, leadership roles, and fellowships. What they receive in the way of experiential learning are connections to the greater community, immeasurable personal growth, and professional growth and development. Public service and citizenship assist student learning and development and increase life skills (Astin, 1999). Service and civic involvement lead students to become involved in the democratic process and enhance leadership skills. Through the incorporation of academic and experiential learning, education occurs on many levels and in many different arenas. In being good citizens, institutions of higher education must give something back to the greater community.

Colleges are places where students "search for identity and meaning . . . . to go beyond their private interest, learn more about the world around them, develop a sense of civic and social responsibility, and discover how they can contribute to the common good" (Boyer, 1997, p. 58). Astin (1995) suggests that for students to acquire the democratic values of honesty, tolerance, empathy, generosity, teamwork, and social responsibility, those qualities must be demonstrated not only through individual professional conduct but in policies and practices. Now more than ever, universities are challenged to educate leaders for the future. The struggle for resources often overshadows the priority of building leadership and civic-minded students, faculty, and staff.

The academy can only gain through community engagement by applying intellectual pursuits to addressing social and community needs. Scholarship must become committed to the engagement. Boyer's work sheds light on the vision of increasing student involvement and the quality of the learning experience. There should be rewards for students, balanced with rewards for faculty for their service as well as for their research and literary pursuits. A culture of engagement should be the focus of a new commitment to students, faculty, staff, and a democratic society (Boyer, 1997).

Astin and Astin (1996), in the social change model, stress the importance of promoting the values of equity, social justice, self-knowledge, personal empowerment, collaboration, citizenship, and service in building future student leaders. Service is a powerful vehicle for developing student leader capabilities. Learning is the result not only of scholarly studies but of life experiences that foster growth, development, and self-knowledge. Oberst (1996) argues that colleges should provide civic education programs that focus on government, public policy, and contemporary issues.

Colleges and universities have access to individuals during years when understanding and enduring attitudes and beliefs about society are formed. Students and faculty are provided with educational opportunities in community service through programs such as faculty in residence, service learning, mentorship, volunteerism, internships, practicums, field experience, and projects that incorporate campus community collaborations with learning. Optimally, a model that incorporates public service, citizenship, and academics would include: collaboration between institutions of higher education and community organizations, experiential student learning, and opportunities for self-awareness and personal growth (Astin, 1999).

Community service is effective as a civic and academic pedagogy (Mabry, 1998). Barber (1994) stresses that civic education in all forms must be an inherent part of liberal studies and that community service must assist students in taking leadership roles in their communities. College student volunteerism intensifies the integration of learning and development, increasing: cognitive development, applied knowledge, engagement, citizenship, and critical thinking (Eyler and Giles, 1999). Marotta and Nashman (1998) propose "that volunteer activity serve as a conduit between academic learning and life experience to produce good citizenship skills" (p. 19).

Students who are involved in service will gain a respect for differences and a willingness to take responsibility in a diverse society. The value of service is taught through modeling and mentorship and through experiential and academic learning. These lessons require a commitment from the community and all other institutional components. A commitment of resources, scholarship, and engagement is required to instill values of service, citizenship, and dedication to a democratic society where all diverse voices have validity and are heard.

The curriculum can enhance student learning by incorporating required community work. Volunteering or serving the community is one way to respond to social need while enhancing the strength of academic learning, life experience, and skills to produce civic-minded individuals. It forces individuals to go beyond their interpersonal world to formulate empathy and understanding of others who may be different from them, thus building community connections and teaching about community organization, leadership, and group dynamics—precious and priceless life lessons. In a pluralistic society, community service fosters citizens' commitment to social good.

Service learning is another way students can engage in learning and service. Experiential learning is combined with classroom learning. Students assume service assignments in the community and have the opportunity for reflection in the classroom. Scholarship is connected to experiential learning; as a result, students are assisted in integrating knowledge experienced in the community with theories and academic-based learning, thus increasing the student's ability for critical thinking and decision making. A greater focus is placed on the scholarship of service as a device to bring about social change. Collaborative relationships between higher education and community organizations can improve the relationships between universities and the communities in which they function. Resources of both community organizations and universities can in this way be used for the maximum benefit of all.

"Community relationships provide evidence of Institutionalization when agency resources are coupled with those of the academy to build reciprocal, enduring, and diverse partnerships that mutually support community interests and academic goals" (Bringle and Hatcher, 2000, p. 275). Through these methods of combining classroom, service, and experiential learning, the specialization hopes to contribute to the development of tomorrow's citizens and leaders.

Having an Impact on the Campus Community

The specialization has influenced the campus, the community, and other universities that accept specialization students for field assignments. The reception has been exceptional in that all entities have been accepting of this new hybrid of student affairs personnel. Guests at the Annual Student-Community Wellness Leadership Symposium have been impressed by both the specialization and its students. Several of the guests have invited students to visit their institutions and have even offered them professional positions in offices of student affairs as a result of the symposium. Students attended and presented at a race relations conference that highlighted campus relations.

SUNY at Stony Brook has utilized specialization students on campus committees, and specialization students have coordinated the university's yearly student, faculty, and staff retreat. Specialization students have championed community service and work hard to maintain visible positions of leadership. They have presented at the professional conferences of the American College Personnel Association (ACPA) and the National Association of Student Personnel Administrators (NASPA), focusing on their professional development in the changing landscapes of college campuses. Graduates of the specialization occupy positions in colleges and universities from New York to California.

To date, we have not conducted a full assessment of the student-community specialization and its effectiveness. In the sixth year of the specialization, plans are under way to assess effectiveness. Recently, the School of Social Welfare underwent accreditation, which it passed for the next eight years. The years prior to the accreditation were focused on the self-study and did not allow for an in-depth examination of the specialization.

An ongoing concern has been leadership. There have been five directors and many changes in faculty since the conception of the specialization. Gaps in leadership have been problematic and have led to decreases in student enrollment. Future goals include thorough assessment using surveys of graduates, employer universities, faculty, and current students to evaluate the effectiveness of the curriculum, goal attainment, and continued mandate for this program.

Future Goals

Future goals of the specialization are to continue to keep student learning and professional preparation at the forefront of the program and the university's mission. We desire to maintain seamless learning for students so that they always understand that we are all holders of knowledge and that by working together we all benefit. We want to continue to help students understand that learning occurs in many different arenas, not only in hallowed halls of the academe.

The specialization will continue to strive to maintain a balanced partnership in collaboration between academic and student affairs in guiding the direction and mission of the specialization. We must develop assessment methods to ensure that our teaching methods are most effective and that our graduates have benefited from this innovative education. Other goals for the specialization include: outcome assessment, a focus on student and community research, student tracking and formalized recruitment, and contributions to the literature.

> This nontraditional program has built a collaborative relationship not only between Student Affairs and Social

Welfare but also between the campus community and surrounding communities. We integrated the two disciplines teaching future campus administrators to focus on community organization, social justice, cultural diversity and student development. This unique partnership prepares students to work on contemporary college campuses with an emphasis on student empowerment and social change, which are vital mechanisms of practice. Students graduate with an ability to respond to a range of issues affecting student communities. The specialization goes a step beyond traditional student affairs programs in addressing the special concerns of individual students and the community that nurtures and sustains them while incorporating principles that value the health and well being of individuals and groups of students as they negotiate the campus community [McDonald and others, 2000, p. 13].

Our main goal is to continue to increase students' understanding of their place in the entire community and the role they play as citizens of a global society.

References

Astin, A. W. (1995). What higher education can do in the cause of citizenship. *Chronicle of Higher Education*, B6.

Astin, A. W. (1999). Promoting leadership, service and democracy. In R. G. Bringle, R. Games, & E. A. Malloy (Eds.), *Colleges and universities as citizens*. Needham Heights, MA: Allyn & Bacon.

Astin, H. S., & Astin, A. W. (1996). *A social change model of leadership development*. Los Angeles: UCLA Higher Education Research Institute.

Bacon, J. B., Velazquez, S., & Wells, R. (2000). Student-community development specialization policy manual. Internal document. State University of New York at Stony Brook, School of Social Welfare.

Bacon, J. L. (2000, August). Promoting citizenship and service in higher education. Paper presented to the Oxford International Round Table on Residential Colleges, Oxford, England.

Barber, B. R. (1994). A proposal for mandatory citizen education and community service. *Michigan Journal of Community Service Learning, 1*(1), 86–93.

Bellah, R. N., Madsen, R., Sullivan, W. M., Swidler, A., & Tipton, S. M. (1996). *Habits of the heart: Individualism and commitment in American life.* Los Angeles: University of California Press.

Boyer, E. L. (1990). *Campus life: In search of community.* Princeton, NJ: Princeton University Press.

Boyer, E. L. (1997). The scholarship of engagement. *Journal of Public Service and Outreach, 1*(1), 11–20.

Bringle, R. G., & Hatcher, J. A. (2000). Institutionalization of service learning in higher education. *The Journal of Higher Education, 71*(3), 715–717.

Eyler, J., & Giles, D. E., Jr. (1999). *Where's the learning in service-learning?* San Francisco: Jossey-Bass.

Mabry, J. B. (1998). Pedagogical variations in service-learning and student outcomes: How time, contact, and reflection matter. *Michigan Journal of Community Service Learning, 5,* 32–47.

Marotta, S., & Nashman, H. (1998). The generation X college student and their motivation for community service. *College Student Affairs Journal, 17*(2) 18–31.

McDonald, W. M., Bacon, J. L., Brown, C. E., Carter, A. W., Littleton, R. A., Moore, B. L., Roper, L. D., & Tankersley, E. (2000). *Collaboration and community: Boyer's guiding principles.* Washington, DC: NASPA Publications.

Oberst, G. (1996). *Building citizenship leaders.* Position paper. Gulf Coast Community College, Panama City, FL.

State University of New York at Stony Brook (2000). School of social welfare application guidebook and application. Author.

Stein, J., Preston, F., Goldstein, M., & Segall, J. (1997). *Community development: Cycle of engagement.* Unpublished document. State University of New York at Stony Brook.

7

Absent Voices

Assessing Students' Perceptions of Campus Community

William M. McDonald

The preceding chapters demonstrate how colleges and universities have struggled with creating a sense of campus community. Inspired by Boyer's vision of community, these institutions labored to create programs and activities that reflect the six principles articulated in *Campus Life: In Search of Community*. And yet students, as a critical group of stakeholders, have not been given a voice in how campus community should be developed and nurtured.

This chapter explores the need for assessing students' perceptions of campus community. Student issues such as how they view and understand the concept of campus community are explored. Further, the chapter reviews a national study of 445 students at 16 institutions demonstrating that institutional variables such as institutional mission, size, and location have an impact on students' perceptions of community.

The Need to Assess Students' Perceptions of Campus Community

Johnetta Brazzell (2001) states that today's students are seeking more than just an academic education when they select a college or university. In fact, whether they realize it or not, they are searching for a community in which they will have a sense of belonging and connection to the overall campus community. If community is not found, "it may prompt some [students] to abandon either their institutions—or worse—their education" (p. 31).

It is not surprising that students are seeking community. Colleges and universities have historically presented their having a strong sense of community as one of many factors for students to consider when selecting an institution. Further, higher education leaders and agencies have focused the nation's attention on the declining state of campus community for the past fifteen years. Bellah and others (1985), Boyer (1987, 1990), Palmer (1981, 1993, 1998), and Zemsky (1993), among many others, have demonstrated that the need to create community is one of the greatest challenges colleges and universities face.

Levine and Cureton (1998) believe these problems of the recent past are further amplified because of the different pressures that current students have faced prior to arriving on campus. "The inescapable conclusion is that today's college students grew up in a time in which everything around them appeared to be changing— and often not for the better. They came of age in that environment without the traditional protection and cushion that the family, church, schools, and youth groups offered their predecessors" (pp. 15–16).

In addition, Shapiro and Levine (1999) note that these students "reflect a greater diversity of experience, ethnicity, expectations, and preparedness than ever before, and institutions need to be ready to face the challenges these students bring with them" (p. 2). Given these student characteristics, as well as the national community debate, it is fair to ask how colleges and universities are assessing students' perceptions of community in order to help students find a sense of belonging and connection.

A student's characterization of campus community (as either strong or weak) is formed from a wide variety of factors that affect the student's sense of connectedness to the campus. The institution can easily anticipate many of these factors. For example, the relationship that the student develops with the mission and purpose of the institution, as well as the relationships developed among fellow students, staff, and faculty, may have a significant impact on the student's personal development and well-being while in college. Further, the degree to which the student understands and supports the institution's traditional and celebrative activities, as well as its future visions and developments, may directly affect the student's satisfaction with his or her sense of connectedness to the institution over time.

Eric Dey (1993) notes, however, that the fragmentation of campus community for students has generated more talk than action. Alexander Astin (1993) agrees and warns that "there is a significant price to be paid, in terms of the student's affective and cognitive development, when there is a low level of student community on the campus" (p. 13). If higher education values community, then students must become participants in the dialogue because they are key campus constituents affected by the declining state of community on the campus. Otherwise, the institution's potential to create community will not be realized. Assessment strategies must be established to assess the effectiveness of an institution's efforts to create community for students. The College and University Community Inventory (CUCI) was created for such a purpose.

The CUCI

Most discussion of the need to create campus community has focused primarily on faculty and administration, who are obviously key, as faculty and administration will probably serve as campus leaders to initiate community. However, campus community will not be accomplished without having students actively engaged in the community-building process. Parker Palmer (1981) reminds us that the institution should "teach [all of us] to be supportive of and accountable to one another; to deal creatively with competing interests; and understand [after all], that we are all in this together" (p. 79).

In an attempt to gain insight into students' perceptions of community, the author (McDonald, 1996, 1999) created the CUCI and used it to conduct a study of 445 students at 16 institutions across the nation. The purpose of the study was to measure the extent and degree of student community within colleges and universities and investigate potential differences in student responses based on institutional variables such as mission, size, and location. Specifically, the study was designed to discover how students understand the concept of community. What features and experiences of their campus life have the greatest value in generating a sense of community among students? Will students' experiences and perceptions differ across institutional types and across regions? What factors might account for those differences if they exist?

The CUCI defines *community* as the policies and practices that mark the distinctive mission of a collegiate institution and that accent the shared values and commitments held in common by institutional constituents. The CUCI is divided into six categories: Mission and Curriculum, Membership Rights and Responsibilities, Respect for Diversity and Individuality, Standards and Regulations, Service to Both Students and Community, and Institutional Rituals and Celebrations. To help students identify their responses, a Likert Scale was provided with the following five responses: disagree = 1, somewhat disagree = 2, neutral = 3, somewhat agree = 4, agree = 5. A narrative copy of the CUCI used in the national study may be reviewed in Exhibit 7.1.

The categories may be divided into two groups. The first group requests information about the practices of community that the institution establishes among its members. Such practices demonstrate the institution's commitment to articulating a vision of institutional mission and purpose and the ceremonies celebrated to reinforce shared purpose among its members. This group includes: Institutional Mission and Curriculum, and Institutional Rituals and Celebrations.

The second group requests information about the relationships of community that the institution establishes among its members.

Exhibit 7.1. The CUCI Scales and Questions

Institutional Mission and Curriculum. My College:

1. commits to academic excellence in education?
2. engages students through teaching/intellectual activities with faculty?
3. creates a supportive environment for student learning?
4. provides opportunities to bring the entire campus together?
5. connects student experiences inside and outside of class?
6. has a well-planned core curriculum?
7. has a well-defined and published set of core values?

Institutional Membership Rights and Responsibilities. My College:

8. encourages freedom of speech/written expression as an institutional value?
9. encourages students to speak and listen to one another carefully?
10. creates an environment where students, faculty, and staff trust one another?
11. allows offensive language/behavior that inhibits student learning?
12. encourages understanding/acceptance of individual differences?
13. creates a climate of civility/protects dignity of students, faculty, and staff?

Institutional Respect for Diversity and Individuality. My College:

14. rejects prejudicial practices/judgments and maintains a fair environment?
15. has stated goals for minority student enrollment?
16. encourages social and educational programming for all students?
17. defines student responsibility for creating a civil environment?
18. supports organizations that are exclusive in membership?
19. aggressively pursues institutional diversity as a model for society?

Institutional Standards and Regulations. My College:

20. expects high standards of student conduct inside/outside the classroom?
21. effectively addresses criminal acts committed by students?
22. encourages students to adopt effective decision-making skills?

Exhibit 7.1. The CUCI Scales and Questions, Cont'd.

23. involves students in creation and evaluation of institutional policy?
24. provides appropriate investigation procedures and review boards?
25. encourages students to acknowledge their obligations to campus community?
26. encourages faculty/staff to model institutional values in their lives?

Institutional Service to both Students and Community. My College:
27. encourages faculty and students to build supportive relationships?
28. addresses student needs through appropriate academic services?
29. encourages students to balance loyalty between groups and college mission?
30. encourages student to connect academic pursuits to everyday life?
31. encourages students and faculty to provide community service?
32. encourages faculty to exhibit a personal concern for students?

Institutional Rituals and Celebrations. My College:
33. shares its history and purpose with students?
34. provides activities to celebrate its heritage?
35. celebrates accomplishments of institution and its members?
36. conducts ceremonies/activities to connect students to institutional constituents?
37. respects the heritage of students and exhibits commitment to diversity?

Source: Adapted from McDonald, 1999, pp. 54–55.

Such relationships demonstrate the individual's level of engagement with the institution, as well as other institution constituents. This group includes: Institutional Membership and Responsibilities, Institutional Respect for Diversity and Individuality, Institutional Standards and Regulations, and Institutional Service to both the Students and Community.

Prior to the CUCI's implementation, student focus groups and a panel of national experts reviewed the instrument. The student

focus groups were conducted at institutions having similar characteristics to the sixteen institutions that participated in the study.
Specifically, the 1987 Carnegie classifications were used to differ-
entiate among institutions. The Carnegie Classification Report
groups colleges and universities in the United States into categories
based on the range of prebaccalaureate to doctorate degrees offered
and the comprehensiveness of the institutional mission. These categories were used in the study:

Research University I and II

Comprehensive University and College I

Comprehensive University and College II

Two-Year Community, Junior and Technical Colleges

Expert panelists were chosen from their respective fields. Participating panelists were: Robert Bellah, Ford Professor of Sociology at the University of California, Berkeley; Alexander Astin,
professor of higher education and director of the Higher Education
Research Institute at the University of California, Los Angeles;
Marvin Peterson, professor of education and director of the Center
for the Study of Higher and Postsecondary Education at the University of Michigan; Carolyn Griswold, responding for Cameron
Fincher, Regents' Professor of Higher Education and Psychology and
director of the Institute of Higher Education at the University of
Georgia; and Ernest Boyer, president of The Carnegie Foundation
for the Advancement of Teaching.

Both groups interpreted the meaning of each question to ensure
that all questions were explicit and elicited an appropriate response.
They recommended modifications, such as additions to or deletions
of existing questions and categories in the CUCI.

To conduct the national test, clusters of four institutions in different geographical regions (Northeast, Southeast, Midwest, and
West) represented the aforementioned 1987 Carnegie classifications

and either small or large (as defined by the author) institutions (small = 3,999 and below; large = 4,000 and above).

Three measurements were used to analyze the data gathered from the national study. First, central tendency measures were calculated to determine students' responses to all questions. Then an analysis of variance (ANOVA) measured any significant differences among students' responses for each question, based on their institutional characteristics of location, size, and Carnegie classification. Finally, after significant differences had been identified, additional ANOVAs were run to determine the specific institutions where those differences were located.

CUCI Findings

A number of significant differences were found among students from institutions representing different regions of the country, different sizes, and different Carnegie classifications. Location resulted in the most significant differences, with 81 percent of the questions identifying significant differences among student responses. The institution's size caused the least impact, with only 27 percent of the questions identifying significant differences among students' responses. Finally, the institution's Carnegie classification caused the second highest number of significant differences; 51 percent of the questions identify significant differences among students' responses.

Regional Location

With regard to location, students from the Southeast scored consistently higher than students in the other regions. Table 7.1 shows the impact of location on students' perceptions of community.

The responses of students from the Southeast affirmed that their institutions' community practices included articulating a shared vision of institutional mission and purpose that had an impact on their daily lives. Further, Southeast students' responses demonstrated that their institutions maintained traditional ceremonies, as

Table 7.1. CUCI Scores by Region

Section	Description	NE	SE	MW	West	Significance
1	Mission & Curriculum		27.26	24.72		P. 000
			27.26		25.53	P. 028
2	Rights & Responsibilities	21.96	23.38			P. 014
		21.96		20.80		P. 058
			23.38	20.80		P. 000
				20.80	23.05	P. 001
3	Diversity & Individuality	19.77	21.68			P. 002
			21.68	19.39		P. 001
				19.39	20.95	P. 035
4	Standards & Regulations	25.27	27.06			P. 017
		25.27		22.86		P. 002
		25.27			23.36	P. 015
			27.06	22.86		P. 000
			27.06		23.36	P. 000
5	Service to Students & Community	22.15		19.63		P. 001
			22.88	19.63		P. 000
				19.63	21.64	P. 022
6	Rituals & Celebrations	16.39	20.14			P. 000
			20.14	16.40		P. 000
			20.14		16.97	P. 000

well as created new activities that reinforced the shared institutional purpose among institutional constituents. As for community relationships, Southeast students' responses indicated that their institution set high standards for their involvement and afforded them responsibilities and rights as community members. In addition, Southeast students' responses indicated that their institutions addressed the needs and goals of all students and provided for the well-being of students and the surrounding community.

Students from the Midwest scored the lowest of all regions on all but one section: Institutional Rituals and Celebrations. With few exceptions, Midwest students' responses were consistently neutral concerning their institution's efforts to establish community practices or relationships.

Finally, depending on the section of the CUCI, students' responses from the Northeast and West alternated between second and third highest. However, the scores from these two regions varied little. Overall, these students' responses were not as affirming as the students' responses from the Southeast. Yet they did support their institution's community practices and relationships more than the Midwest students' responses indicate.

Institutional Size

When considering institutional size, students' responses from large and small institutions alternated between high and low, depending on the section of the CUCI. (Table 7.2 identifies the impact of institutional size on students' perceptions of community.) Overall, however, students from small institutions scored higher on the majority of the questions. The responses of students from small schools affirmed that their institution's mission and purpose affected them daily. Students' responses from large schools were neutral and did not indicate such an impact in their lives. Likewise, students from small institutions affirmed their institution's efforts to provide for the well-being of students and the surrounding community. Students from large institutions remained neutral.

Table 7.2. CUCI Scores by Institutional Size

Section	Description	Large	Small	Significance
1	Mission & Curriculum	25.20	26.35	P. 004
5	Service to Students & Community	20.52	22.39	P. 002

The responses of students from institutions of both sizes were very similar for the remaining sections. As for the institution's ability to afford students community rights and responsibilities, meet the needs of all students, provide clear expectations, and provide activities that reinforce the shared purpose among institutional members, students from both large and small institutions were generally neutral.

Carnegie Classification

Finally, students from Comprehensive Universities and Colleges scored highest on the majority of the test. (Table 7.3 identifies the impact of Carnegie classification on students' perceptions of community.) Students from both types of institutions consistently affirmed their institution's efforts to establish community practices and relationships. The mission and purpose of these institutions affected the lives of their students daily.

Likewise, these students' responses affirmed that Comprehensive Universities and Colleges afforded students rights and responsibilities, addressed the needs and goals of all students, placed expectations on students, provided for the well-being of students and surrounding community, and maintained traditional ceremonies and activities to reinforce a shared purpose among all members.

Students' responses from Research Universities scored third highest; those from Two-Year institutions scored lowest. Students' responses from these institutions were more neutral when describing the community practices and relationships on campus.

Table 7.3. CUCI Scores by Carnegie Classification

Section	Description	Research University	Comprehensive University	Comprehensive College	Two-Year School	Significance
1	Mission & Curriculum	24.56	26.44			P. 005
		24.56		27.14		P. 000
				27.14	25.27	P. 025
3	Diversity & Individuality	19.80	21.41			P. 008
			21.41		19.81	P. 029
5	Service to Students & Community	19.58	22.25			P. 000
		19.58		23.25		P. 000
		19.58			21.42	P. 039
				23.25	21.42	P. 029
6	Rituals & Celebrations		17.73		15.99	P. 022
				18.44	15.99	P. 001

CUCI Conclusions

It was reasonable to have anticipated differences among students' responses to campus community practices and relationships based on institutional variables such as the regional location, size, and Carnegie classification. However, the number and type of differences could not have reasonably been anticipated. For example, it was surprising that students from the Southeast consistently scored higher than students from other regions. Likewise, it was surprising to see that students from the Midwest scored consistently lower than students in other regions. One reason for this may have been the physical location of the participating institutions. For example, institutions from the Southeast were located in more rural and small-town locations. Institutions from the Midwest were located in smaller cities and in suburban and urban areas. In addition, the institutions from the Southeast had more involved and better-known athletic programs than those from other regions. Students may identify athletic events with a sense of connectedness with the institution.

With regard to size, it was surprising to see that students from small schools did not score significantly higher than their large-school counterparts. The recruiting material from most small colleges claims that small schools are more effective than large schools at establishing community relationships and practices. The results from this national survey do not support such a generalization. However, it would be a mistake to totally discount the impact of institutional size on students' perceptions of community. The results of this study indicate that the arbitrary size differences imposed by the author were not effective in distinguishing differences in students' perceptions. And yet the 1987 Carnegie classification variable, of which institutional size was a distinguishing characteristic, did solicit a number of significant differences among students' perceptions of community.

With regard to Carnegie classification, it was not surprising that Comprehensive Universities and Colleges scored higher than Research Universities and Two-Year schools. Comprehensive Universities and Colleges usually place more emphasis on undergraduate teaching than Research Universities do. Students at Two-Year schools consistently scored the lowest of all other classifications. Reasons entail outside variables in these students' lives such as work, family, and other factors that may require more time than attending class at a Two-Year school. In addition, students at Two-Year schools are generally commuter students who do not participate in cocurricular activities.

Finally, a host of other variables may affect the students' perceptions of community within their institution. These variables are more individual in nature. For example, individual differences such as students' classification, years enrolled, residence status, age, gender, academic major, and ethnicity have as much potential to affect students' perceptions of community as the institutional variables of regional location, size, and Carnegie classification. The correlation of these variables in influencing students' perceptions of community requires further study.

These variables (institutional or individual demographics) are not inherently community promoters or detractors. They are, however, factors that a college or university must consider carefully if it is trying to increase the effectiveness of its community practices and relationships in order to strengthen the students' sense of connectedness with the institution.

Suggestions for Future Research

As indicated in the previous section, the CUCI has a number of implications for higher education. Future applications will produce more information about students' perceptions of community on their campus, which colleges and universities may use to provide better learning experiences and services. However, a number of corrections to the design of the study need to made in future research involving the CUCI (McDonald, 1998).

CUCI Modifications

In the original design, *community* was defined as the set of policies and practices that mark the distinctive mission of a collegiate institution and that accent the shared values and commitments held in common by institutional constituents. Community included the following scales: Mission and Curriculum, Membership Rights and Responsibilities, Respect for Diversity and Individuality, Standards and Regulations, Service to Both Students and Community, and Rituals and Celebrations. Yet, as discovered during the study, the physical location of the campus may affect both institutional and individual demographic variables that could influence students' perceptions of community (see Exhibit 7.2 to review the revised [1998] CUCI).

A new scale must be created and added to the instrument. The section titled "Institutional Physical Location and Interaction" contains questions that address institutional variables such as whether the institution is located in a rural, small town, small city, suburban, or urban setting. Additional questions relate to the physical layout of the campus and its impact on students' perceptions of community. For example, are there spaces in the buildings and on the grounds that allow for both formal and informal gatherings of faculty, staff, and students? Are there barriers such as major streets, railways, or waterways that detract from the physical attributes of the community? Finally, are curricular and cocurricular facilities designed in a manner to engage students with other constituents of the campus?

Also, as technology continues to advance rapidly, a new CUCI scale to measure the impact of technology will be required. Some of these concerns may be addressed in this new section. For example, most institutions are experiencing rapid changes in technological advances. The creation of computer networks such as the

Exhibit 7.2. College and University Community Inventory

The CUCI is designed to assess individual students' perceptions of community with his/her college or university. Community is defined as the set of policies and practices that mark the distinctive mission of a collegiate institution and that accent the shared values and commitments held in common by institutional constituents. Please read all instructions carefully and answer questions accordingly. Responses will enable your college to better create and nurture campus community.

Part 1.   Please share information that applies to you by circling the appropriate response; when appropriate, fill in the corresponding blank.

1.   My classification is:
- a.) freshman
- b.) sophomore
- c.) junior
- d.) senior
- e.) graduate
- f.) part-time

2.   Years I have attended:
- a.) 0–1
- b.) 2–3
- c.) 4–5
- d.) 6 or more

3.   My housing status is:
- a.) on campus residence
- b.) off campus residence

4.   My age is:
- a.) 15–19
- b.) 20–29
- c.) 30–39
- d.) 40 or more

5.   My gender is:
- a.) female
- b.) male

6.   My academic major is:
- a.) Business
- b.) Education
- c.) Engineering
- d.) Humanities
- e.) Physical Science
- f.) Social Science
- g.) Other (specify: _____)

7.   My ethnicity is:
- a.) African-American
- b.) American Indian
- c.) Asian
- d.) Caucasian
- e.) Hispanic
- f.) Other (specify: _____)

Part 2.   Please read the description for each section. For each statement, choose a response for your institution and circle the corresponding number. Following are the responses:

0	1	2	3	4
Not Observed	Strongly Disagree	Disagree	Agree	Strongly Agree
(NO)	(SD)	(D)	(A)	(SA)

Exhibit 7.2. College and University Community Inventory, Cont'd.

INSTITUTIONAL MISSION AND CURRICULUM: Consider the purpose and mission of your institution and how it impacts students on a daily basis. My college:

		NO	SD	D	A	SA
1.	commits to academic excellence in education?	0	1	2	3	4
2.	engages students through creative teaching/ intellectual activities with faculty?	0	1	2	3	4
3.	creates a supportive environment for student learning?	0	1	2	3	4
4.	provides opportunities bringing entire campus together?	0	1	2	3	4
5.	connects student learning experiences inside and outside of class through programs/activities?	0	1	2	3	4
6.	has a well-planned core curriculum?	0	1	2	3	4
7.	has a well-defined and published set of core values?	0	1	2	3	4

INSTITUTIONAL MEMBERSHIP AND RESPONSIBILITIES: Consider the rights and responsibilities your institution affords students. My college:

		NO	SD	D	A	SA
8.	encourages freedom of speech and written expression as an institutional value?	0	1	2	3	4
9.	encourages students to speak and listen to one another carefully?	0	1	2	3	4
10.	creates and environment where students, faculty and staff trust one another?	0	1	2	3	4
11.	allows offensive language/behavior that inhibits student learning?	0	1	2	3	4
12.	encourages understanding/acceptance of individual differences among students?	0	1	2	3	4
13.	creates a climate of civility and protects dignity of students, faculty and staff?	0	1	2	3	4

INSTITUTIONAL RESPECT FOR DIVERSITY AND INDIVIDUALITY: Consider how your institution addresses the needs and goals of all students. My college:

		NO	SD	D	A	SA
14.	rejects prejudicial practices and judgments and maintains a fair and equitable environment?	0	1	2	3	4
15.	has stated goals for minority student enrollment?	0	1	2	3	4

Exhibit 7.2. College and University Community Inventory, Cont'd.

	NO	SD	D	A	SA
16. encourages social and educational programming for all students?	0	1	2	3	4
17. defines student responsibility for creating a civil environment?	0	1	2	3	4
18. supports organizations that are exclusive in membership?	0	1	2	3	4
19. aggressively pursues institutional diversity as a model for society?	0	1	2	3	4

INSTITUTIONAL STANDARDS AND REGULATIONS: Consider expectations your institution places upon students. My college:

	NO	SD	D	A	SA
20. expects high standards of student conduct inside/outside the classroom?	0	1	2	3	4
21. effectively addresses criminal acts committed by students?	0	1	2	3	4
22. encourages student to adopt effective decision making skills and responsibility for the decisions?	0	1	2	3	4
23. involves students in creation/evaluation of policies and procedures, and codes of student conduct?	0	1	2	3	4
24. provides appropriate investigation procedures and review boards for alleged student violations?	0	1	2	3	4
25. encourages students to acknowledge their obligations to campus community?	0	1	2	3	4
26. encourages faculty/staff to model institutional values in their professional and personal lives?	0	1	2	3	4

INSTITUTIONAL SERVICE TO BOTH STUDENTS AND COMMUNITY: Consider your institution's efforts to provide for the well being of students and surrounding community. My college:

	NO	SD	D	A	SA
27. encourages faculty and students to build supportive relationships?	0	1	2	3	4
28. addresses student needs through appropriate academic services, facility and personnel access?	0	1	2	3	4
29. encourages students to maintain a proper balance of loyalty between groups and college mission?	0	1	2	3	4
30. encourages students to connect academic pursuits to every day life?	0	1	2	3	4

Exhibit 7.2. College and University Community Inventory, Cont'd.

		NO	SD	D	A	SA
31.	encourages students and faculty to provide service to the community?	0	1	2	3	4
32.	encourages faculty to exhibit a personal concern for students?	0	1	2	3	4

INSTITUTIONAL RITUALS AND CELEBRATIONS: Consider your institution's efforts to maintain traditional ceremonies, as well as create new activities to reinforce the shared purpose among members. My college:

		NO	SD	D	A	SA
33.	shares its history and purpose with students?	0	1	2	3	4
34.	provides activities to celebrate its heritage?	0	1	2	3	4
35.	celebrates academic accomplishments of institution, as well as those of faculty, staff and students?	0	1	2	3	4
36.	conducts ceremonies/activities that connect students to alumni, benefactors and retirees?	0	1	2	3	4
37.	respects all students' heritage and demonstrates commitment to diversity through celebrations?	0	1	2	3	4

INSTITUTIONAL PHYSICAL LOCATION AND INTERACTION: Consider your institution's physical location and campus layout. My college:

		NO	SD	D	A	SA
38.	has been located in an appropriate location?	0	1	2	3	4
39.	provides buildings and grounds that facilitate informal gatherings between faculty, staff and students?	0	1	2	3	4
40.	effectively addresses accessibility requirements of all campus members and guests?	0	1	2	3	4
41.	minimizes physical barriers such as major streets, railways or waterways that detracts from the physical attributes of campus community?	0	1	2	3	4
42.	designs facilities to engage students with campus alumni, guests and other constituents?	0	1	2	3	4
43.	maintains appropriate technological advances such as computer networks, multimedia classrooms, use of remote campuses?	0	1	2	3	4

Exhibit 7.2. College and University Community Inventory, Cont'd.

Part 3.   The final section of the CUCI requests general students' perceptions about their college or university's strengths and weaknesses for creating and nurturing campus community. Likewise these final questions may assess students' perceptions of a specific program/project designed to create campus community. Please answer the following two questions.

44.   What is the most important campus attribute for creating and nurturing community on the campus?

45.   What is the greatest detractor for creating and nurturing community on the campus?

Internet and campus e-mail; the development of multimedia classrooms, including teleconferences and phone conferences; and the establishment of remote sites to engage new populations of students have greatly affected students' perceptions of community.

New Student Response Measures

The Likert Scale is effective in quantifying students' responses to survey questions. However, the original placement of the "Neutral" response did not produce useful information. Further, forcing students to choose stronger responses will provide institutions more powerful information for study. A new response, "Not Observed," placed at the beginning of the scale and given the value of zero, will yield a wider variety of answers. The new scale will appear as the following:

0	1	2	3	4
Not Observed	Strongly Disagree	Disagree	Agree	Strongly Agree

Although this quantifiable information is useful, its usefulness may increase with the addition of qualitative measures. Consequently, the following two qualitative questions must be added at the end of the CUCI:

    a. **What is the most important campus attribute for creating and nurturing community on this campus?**

    b. **What is the greatest detractor for creating and nurturing community on this campus?**

Expanded Administration

The next logical step for future study would be a larger field test involving more institutions and different geographical regions. The original national study involved only four types of institutions, as identified by the 1987 Carnegie classifications. Those classifications, however, were modified and expanded in 1994 and again in 2000 by The Carnegie Foundation. In addition to adding new categories to represent an increasing number of higher education institutions, some of the categories were renamed to provide clarity to institutional differences. These new categories offer a wider variety of institutions to be surveyed to evaluate how different types of institutions affect students.

With regard to this study, there is one notable distinction between the old and new Carnegie classifications. In 1987, many classifications made either direct or indirect reference to the size of the institution. For example, both Research University classifications made reference to the number of doctorates conferred and the amount of federal support received. The Comprehensive Universities and Colleges classification made reference to enrollment size. Under the 1994 classifications, however, references to enrollment were deleted. This may have implications if studies are made concerning the impact of institutional size on students' perceptions of community. As this study demonstrates, however, institutional size (at least when arbitrarily set at the aforementioned levels for this study) is not often a significant variable.

Summary and Conclusions

This chapter has demonstrated that there are common descriptors of community among college and university students. From the original focus groups used to build the initial instrument through the field test, students have been able to identify their perceptions of community on their campus. The importance of a sense of connectedness with the institution, its practices, and its relationships varied from student to student in different institutions. For example, at a focus group with a Research Institution, when responding to the meaning of the questions, one student wrote in the margins, "How are students to know what faculty and staff do in their personal life?" This student's question is an important one for campus constituents to answer if the institution intends to foster a sense of connectedness among all community members.

The national debate concerning the need to develop community on campus is as essential today as it was twelve years ago when Boyer (1990) and The Carnegie Foundation published their national survey of college presidents. Yet because of the minimal amount of research assessing the importance of community to students, the role of the student in the debate is at best not widely known. Is a sense of community on campus important to students? Do students desire to feel a sense of connectedness among the many different campus constituents? If so, does a lack of a sense of community affect their actions? Is it important to students to feel a sense of connectedness to the institutional mission and purpose? Finally, does a student's sense of community, or lack thereof, have an impact on the effectiveness and work of the faculty?

The CUCI allows colleges and universities to explore students' perceptions on all of these issues. For institutions striving to build community, student responses to the CUCI will provide an additional assessment of the institution's effectiveness in developing meaningful community relationships and activities for all campus constituents.

In closing, still prevalent on today's campuses are the increasing problems that result from inappropriate student behavior and students' competing interests, ideologies, and purposes, as well as the transient nature of the student population. As this study has demonstrated, students' overall perceptions of community on campus will be affected by institutional characteristics such as size, location, and Carnegie classification. Further, individual student demographic differences may have an impact on the student's overall perceptions of community on campus. However, further research is required to confirm that one way or the other. In either case, students must be brought into the debate. Otherwise, Brazzell's (2001) concern about students abandoning their institutions (a potential consequence if they cannot find a sense of belonging) may become a reality for increasing numbers of colleges and universities.

References

Astin, A. W. (1993, October). Higher education and the concept of community. Fifteenth David Dodds Henry Lecture, University of Illinois at Urbana-Champaign.

Bellah, R. N., Madsen, R., Sullivan, W. M., Swidler, A., & Tipton, S. M. (1985). *Habits of the heart: Individualism and commitment in American life.* Berkeley: University of California Press.

Boyer, E. L. (1987). *College: The undergraduate experience in America.* New York: Harper & Row.

Boyer, E. L. (1990). *Campus life: In search of community.* Princeton, NJ: Princeton University Press.

Brazzell, J. C. (2001, January-February). A sense of belonging. In *About campus: Enriching the student learning experience*, pp. 31–32. San Francisco: Jossey-Bass.

Dey, E. (1993, Spring). What kind of community on campus? In *Planning for Higher Education*, pp. 34–35. Ann Arbor, MI: Society for College and University Planning.

Levine, A., & Cureton, J. S. (1998). *When hope and fear collide: A portrait of today's college student.* San Francisco: Jossey-Bass.

McDonald, W. M. (1996). The College and University Community Inventory: Assessing student perceptions of community in higher education. *Dissertation Abstracts International 58*(6A). (University Microfilms No. 9735340)

McDonald, W. M. (1998). The College and University Community Inventory, Revised.

McDonald, W. M. (1999). The College and University Community Inventory: A new tool to assess students' perceptions of community. *College Student Affairs Journal*, *18*(2), 44–55.

Palmer, P. J. (1981). *The company of strangers: Christians and the renewal of America's public life*. New York: Crossroad.

Palmer, P. J. (1993). Remembering the heart of higher education. From *AAHE's 1993 National Conference on Higher Education*. Washington, DC: American Association of Higher Education.

Palmer, P. J. (1998) *The courage to teach: Exploring the inner landscape of a teacher's life*. San Francisco: Jossey-Bass.

Shapiro, N. S., & Levine, J. H. (1999). *Creating learning communities: A practical guide to winning support, organizing for change, and implementing programs*. San Francisco: Jossey-Bass

Zemsky, R. (Ed.). (1993, November). *Policy Perspectives, 5*, pp. 1A–12A.

8

Conclusion

Final Reflections and Suggestions for Creating Campus Community

William M. McDonald, Jean L. Bacon,
Cathy E. Brown, J. Mark Brown, Arthur W. Carter,
Robert A. Littleton, Betty L. Moore,
Larry D. Roper, and Cynthia A. Wells

Colleges and universities often express the desire to improve the sense of campus community but recognize the obstacles that hinder their following through on their intentions. Community building is difficult work for both the individual and the institution. For the individual, Palmer (1987) writes, "the degree to which the individual yearns for community is directly related to the dimming of memory of his or her last experience of it" (p. 20). For the institution, Robert Zemsky (1993) states that a consistent challenge voiced by colleges and universities is the loss of campus community.

Reflections and Insights

Each of the five participating institutions identified in this book, regardless of enrollment, institutional mission, or affiliation, speak to the challenge of building community.

This chapter draws together our reflections and the insights we gained from our efforts to build community on our five respective campuses. Each institution was asked to answer four questions, which we discuss next. And we hope the answers they gave will guide similar institutions in their efforts to identify their own obstacles to and opportunities for creating campus community.

1. *What do you know now that you wish you had known when you began your community-building initiative?*

The crucial step for community building is identifying a core group of people committed to a shared vision. Both the group and the vision are equally important. The group must develop relationships built on trust and open communication. Members must communicate in ways that invite everyone to collaborate in order to achieve more through community than any one individual could alone. Members must exhibit courage and support, accepting failures as well as successes in implementing community-building initiatives. Otherwise, members will not assume the risks inherent in implementing new ideas.

Likewise, the shared vision must inspire passions and commitments among group members. The shared vision must challenge the institution to explore ways in which community building may be sustained. Often building institutional consensus around community building is even more difficult than encouraging members to risk collaborating. A shared vision is necessary to attract new members and to expand the work of community building. Finally, institutions striving to build a stronger sense of community must create a reward structure for faculty, staff, and students involved in these efforts. For faculty and staff, such a structure must include appropriate recognitions (titles, reduced teaching or committee assignments) and rewards (stipends, evaluation). An appropriate student recognition and reward system must also be created.

Community building is both intentional and happenstance, and both should be valued. Campus groups that sponsor programs reflecting their particular interest may advance community among its members. However, groups may also advance community through-out the entire campus. For example, a program sponsored by inter-national students on campus demonstrates a sense of belonging that encourages international students to share their experience. Like-wise, the campus may advance community for all students by spon-soring international programming that engages all students, faculty, and staff. Both demonstrate community building. However, if one is present and the other is not, it may point to issues that need to be addressed in order to broaden community.

2. What have been the obstacles to community-building efforts?

One obstacle when attempting community building is a shared misunderstanding of what community means. Usually, there is no common, agreed-upon definition of community. Often campus con-stituents define community in speech or practice in fundamentally different ways. If community is to suggest anything more than a warm and fuzzy feeling, a common definition should be identified and quantified to justify the expenditure of personnel and financial resources.

Another obstacle is the constantly changing nature of the cam-pus population. Colleges and universities experience a constant transition in faculty, staff, and students. Consequently, in order for community-building initiatives to be sustained, the shared vision must be passed from one generation to another. Experienced mem-bers will leave the community; new members will bring ideas that may or may not connect neatly to the existing community-building initiative. The community issues to be addressed will change as the population changes—an obstacle that is mitigated by community-building initiatives that focus on real issues and real problems.

Finally, and as previously noted, the institution must allocate sufficient resources to accomplish the goals of the community-building work. Both personnel and financial resources reflect that the institution values the community-building projects.

3. What is the most significant contribution your program has made to your institution?

The most significant contribution for all five campuses has been the creation of a common language of community that is easily understood by faculty, staff, and students. This language has created a new civility that allows participants to interact in more meaningful ways than other programs or activities on campus. Conflicts become more constructive. Goals are more clearly defined, and participants say their sense of belonging at the institution has been increased by participating in the community-building initiative.

On most of the campuses, this common language of community has facilitated a spirit of interdependence that has spilled onto other areas of the campus. Participants invite colleagues or fellow students to participate in specific activities. Once introduced, students may look for future opportunities to participate in specific community-building initiatives.

4. What is the next step for your community-building initiative?

Without exception, each of the five participating institutions indicated a desire to expand their program to involve more campus members. Another common concern was developing better assessment strategies for gauging the impact of their community-building initiative. Following are their answers.

Carson-Newman College

During the 2001 spring semester, the Leadership Team led focus group discussions with current Boyer Fellows. From these discussions, a redesign of the Boyer Laboratory for Learning has been created and will be implemented during the 2001-02 academic year. Six teams will be reduced to two, and neither team will be affiliated with a residence hall. Teams will be gender-specific in that they will be made up of all women or all men and will provide programming for specific male or female issues and interests. Both teams will collaborate to provide programming around a central theme—one that connects classroom learning with out-of-class learning and builds campus community among all faculty, staff, and students. A new Boyer Fellow, solely responsible for expanding our assessment strategies, will be secured as part of the Leadership Team. Finally, a new group of students called Boyer Scholars will be recruited to participate in the Boyer Laboratory for Learning. Although the Boyer Scholars will not be part of the Boyer Teams, they will attend Boyer Laboratory activities and serve as a critical mass of students to be strategically assessed to better understand the impact of the program on the larger student body.

Messiah College

The most critical step will be to involve a broader population of the campus in their existing community-building initiatives. A specific concern is analyzing the state of community for faculty and staff at the college. To accomplish this, a campuswide summit for discussing community on campus will be held. It is hoped that this conversation will enhance the college's efforts to identify real or perceived obstacles and agendas and address them to keep these obstacles from blocking community-building initiatives.

Oregon State University

The next step is to design educational and interpersonal interactions in a manner that ensures the humanity and dignity of every person (whether or not that person is involved in a community-building initiative) is protected. For example, the Division of Student Affairs has created an institutional diversity initiative (based on the National Coalition Building Institute's model) and is providing leadership for implementing the initiative campuswide with different departments and campus groups.

Penn State University

The next step will be to continue to encourage staff to develop community-building initiatives and associated learning outcomes as part of their strategic planning efforts. Another step is to link program assessment that illustrates the contributions of community-building efforts to cement the importance of shaping the out-of-classroom experiences of the thousands of students who attend the university.

SUNY at Stony Brook

An institutionwide plan has been developed to broaden the community-building initiatives by addressing specific needs of faculty, staff, and student constituent groups. The campus environment will be restructured to create centers for each constituent group. As a whole, the centers will expand community programming, create new traditions, provide cross-cultural experiences, and initiate facility improvements to build a stronger sense of respect and interdependence among all community members.

Concluding Comments: Creating Campus Community

In conclusion, community building, whether at a large research university with decentralized units and multiple campuses or a small liberal arts college, requires paying special attention to the unique set of needs and concerns expressed by the faculty, staff, students, and administrators involved in the process. Otherwise, the complexity of trying to encourage such diverse constituents to commit to applying one vision may be overwhelming.

As we have demonstrated, community can be an elusive concept. The term *community* means different things to different people and hardly ever the same thing to any two people. And even though defining the term is a difficult task, *achieving* community is even more challenging. Developing community at a college or university is made more difficult because of the dynamic and changing nature of the population; members flow in and out of the campus constantly. This transition in community membership means that campus community-building efforts will experience constant disruption as a result of losing experienced members and being joined by new members who are not aware of the norms, values, and shared commitments of ongoing community members.

As we have also demonstrated, students must have a voice in how colleges and universities create a sense of community. This will only happen when colleges and universities actively assess student perceptions of community on campus. Any discussion of community without student involvement will be problematic because key constituents will not be represented in the community-building process.

If we are to build community among students, faculty, and staff at a college and university, our efforts to build bridges must be focused, ongoing, and comprehensive. As demonstrated by Ernest L. Boyer Sr., building community involves bridging ideas and relationships that are life-giving, life-affirming, and life-sustaining. Boyer (1990) writes:

> What is needed, we believe, is a larger, more integrative vision of community in higher education, one that focuses not on the length of time students spend on campus, but on the quality of the encounter, and relates not only to social activities, but to the classroom, too. The goal as we see it is to clarify both academic and civic standards, and above all, to define with some precision the enduring values that undergird a community of learning [p. 7].

How do we go about building bridges to create such community on our campuses? We believe that the following seven activities will help.

1. Create clear and elevating goals—define the "big picture" work of the organization.

2. Engage members in charting the direction of the organization—personalize the organization's work by increasing the investment of individual members.

3. Reduce anonymity by facilitating members learning each others' names—work against isolation.

4. Agree on conversation ground rules—develop a culture of civility.

5. Create opportunities for input, feedback, and reflection—create space for the individual "voices" of community members.

6. Develop specific activities that will move the organization toward its community goals—translate your aspirations into concrete work.

7. Periodically review organizational progress—chart the organization's journey and refocus as needed.

These attributes must be present for a sense of community to develop. Among the necessary qualities are such things as these: members know each other by name; participants are open to the beliefs and values of other members; conflict is acknowledged, and there are means by which conflict is resolved; and members celebrate the successes of those within the community. However profound our goals may be, community requires more than merely accomplishing a series of tasks.

To create real community we must act with care. We need to act with passion, with a clear vision, and with thoughtfulness toward others. It should be evident through the behaviors of community members that we are committed to the growth and development of all our members. Community will be achieved through our shared commitment to care for the social, emotional, psychological, intellectual, physical, and spiritual condition of the space we share. As a community, we would make it our responsibility to ensure that the humanity and dignity of each person is preserved and nurtured. We will acknowledge the struggles associated with being human and the limitations that each of us brings to our interactions. The community-building process requires that we design our educational and inter-personal interactions in ways that will facilitate members being able to have meaningful communication with each other. Community members will have opportunities to talk about real issues and work together to solve real problems.

To build a sense of community, we need to act with heart and courage. Community is constructed through encountering and re-solving conflicts. True communities commit to making hard choices. To build community we must take risks with each other. Commu-nity leaders work with members to construct experiences through which members will struggle with each other to identify differences as well as shared commitments.

When we are in community with each other, we need to ac-knowledge our interdependence and shared destiny. In true com-munity, we create the context in which others will feel sustained, nourished, stimulated, engaged, and appreciated. Interdependence means we look for the value in what others bring rather than dwell on what they are lacking. We look for strengths rather than flaws. We pull when needed and push when required, all with the goal of moving our community forward. We rejoice in our journey and in those with whom we share the journey. We demonstrate genuine commitment to take the life situations, aspirations, identities, and needs of community members seriously and support them as they strive to achieve success. Interdependence means when one of us is diminished, we are collectively diminished.

As we work at developing community, we acknowledge the struggles of learning to communicate better and of bringing together people from a broad range of life situations. Community building is hard work. In some ways, it may be the hardest work that some of us will ever attempt. Community building is work of the heart, spirit, and soul. This work requires vulnerability, openness, perseverance, and humility. If we are to build community, our leaders must allow themselves to be fully human and create the space where others' humanity can flourish. In community building, the joy is not in the achievement; the joy is in the struggle—the struggle of always building bridges to make meaning of our collective social and educational experience.

References

Boyer, E. L. (1990). *Campus life: In search of community*. Princeton, NJ: Princeton University Press.

Palmer, P. J. (1987, September-October). Community, conflict, and ways of knowing. *Change, 18,* 20–25.

Zemsky, R. (Ed.). (1993, November). *Policy Perspectives, 5,* 1A–12A.

Afterword

The Quest for Community in Higher Education

Parker J. Palmer

Academic culture is a curious and conflicted thing. On the one hand, it holds out the allure and occasionally the reality of being a "community of scholars"—colleagues with common roots in the depths of the intellectual tradition working together to seek new insights into the world's wonders. On the other hand, it is a culture infamous for fragmentation, isolation, and competitive individualism—a culture in which community sometimes feels harder to come by than in any other institution on the face of the earth.

This cultural contradiction is vexing, partly because people feel resentful when they are promised one thing and given something quite different. When the academy fails to achieve sustained community in even minimal form, its capacity to pursue its core mission is weakened.

That mission can be summed up in three words: *knowing, teaching,* and *learning.* And all three of those words name enterprises that are essentially communal. This claim seems simple and straightforward, but the truth is that we tacitly understand the academy's three-fold mission in highly individualistic terms. Knowing is often regarded as an act of personal genius, something done by very smart people working largely in isolation. Teaching and learning are often regarded as a one-on-one exchange of information, a transfer of knowledge from a teacher who is quite smart to a student who is not—at least not yet!

However, when knowing, teaching, and learning are understood and pursued in these ways, we not only distort intellectual history but we fail to develop genuine intellectual capacity in the next generation. Knowing has always been and always will be a dialectic between individual insight and shared communal understandings—a back-and-forth of dissent and consent around what we see and what it means, without which our sight would be even dimmer than it is. Teaching and learning have always been and always will be a complex dance between teachers, students, and subjects, a communal engagement with each other and with the world without which authentic education cannot happen.

Community in higher education is not optional but essential if we wish to pursue our mission with full integrity. In service of that mission, I want to explore the quest for community on three levels of academic life: community across the entire staff of an institution; community in the classroom and other teaching and learning venues; and community between the academy and the world around it.

Community Across the Staff

I spent my undergraduate years at Carleton College in Minnesota, and among the remarkable teachers I had on that campus were Dacie and Roy Moses. Neither of them had a Ph.D., and I am not even sure whether either of them had graduated from high school. Dacie, who was in her sixties when I was a student, worked behind the desk in the college library. Roy had been a skilled carpenter in his younger years, but early on, while he was helping a neighbor build a barn, a huge beam had fallen on him, leaving Roy permanently disabled and largely homebound.

The Moses' house on the edge of campus was a home-away-from-home for many Carleton undergraduates, including me. If you were having trouble with a professor, trouble with romance, trouble with your parents, or—most likely—trouble with yourself, stopping by Dacie's and Roy's for a round of cribbage, coffee, cookies, and conversation was the best therapy you could get.

In what sense were Dacie and Roy my teachers? What I learned from them was the very incarnation of the abstract ideas we were studying in our liberal arts courses. I learned that generosity is stronger than arrogance. I learned about the dignity of common work. I learned about the value of honest relationships. I learned about the transcendence of the human spirit.

There are many things that make me proud of my alma mater and grateful to her. But nothing makes me prouder or more grateful than the fact that, after Roy and Dacie died, the college purchased their home and turned it into a permanent house of hospitality, honoring the fact that—rightly understood—everyone who works at a college is a teacher.

The notion that "we are all teachers" is not romanticism. Instead, it is a simple reality related to what educational researchers have called the hidden curriculum. What students learn in college comes not only—and certainly not principally—from lectures, readings, and discussions, that is, from the content of the formal curriculum. It comes from the way individual and collective life is lived on a campus—from the way the people employed there do their work, conduct their relationships, make their choices, and otherwise reveal their true values, which may be quite at odds with the values espoused in the classroom.

We should celebrate the congruities we find between academic rhetoric and practice, and we should be conscious and critical of the many incongruities. It is cause for celebration when we teach courses on ecological problems *and* have a buildings and grounds crew that takes leadership in a campus recycling program; when we exhort students to become good citizens *and* have a faculty that conducts its decision making in a civil manner; when we advocate good customer relations in business courses *and* have a registrar's staff that deals understandingly with students when they are trying to enroll in overcrowded courses.

But when we find incongruities at points such as these, we can be sure of one thing: students are learning at least as much from what we do as from what we say. We need to work hard on aligning the hidden curriculum with our educational purposes—as hard as we work on our formal course offerings. Above all, we must work to bring all staff into a shared sense of community and mission, for only so will people be willing to embrace the reality that we are all teachers.

This, in turn, requires a realistic understanding of what community among staff might mean. Every educational institution has gaps, large and small, between administrative, academic, student services, and professional support staff—gaps in power, status, income, job security. Although some of these gaps can and should be narrowed or closed, others will always be with us. Community among staff cannot have a utopian meaning that flies in the face of reality, or the rhetoric will discourage rather than empower people.

So what might community mean in a real-life situation? I believe that certain experiential markers allow individuals to feel that they are in community with others despite any gaps that might exist. Here are five such markers that are within our reach, if we choose to reach for them:

1. I feel in community when I believe that I play a meaningful role in a shared educational mission, and others see me doing so. The first part—belief—is my own responsibility, and it often requires inner work to embrace the meaning of my own role. The second part is the responsibility of others: leaders who articulate the shared mission, staff development activities that assume a shared mission, and colleagues in other departments who act as if we had a shared mission.

2. I feel in community when I am affirmed for the work I do on behalf of the shared mission if it contributes to that mission. If what I do falls short, I am told about that as well and offered help to improve my performance. That is, I am not ignored in either the successes or the failures of the work I do.

3. I feel in community when I know that I can take creative risks in my work and sometimes fail—and still be supported. I un-

derstand that not any old risk will do. The risks must be worth taking to advance the shared mission, and the failures must be such that I can learn from them. But within those limits, the safety to fail in a good cause and still be supported is one of the marks that I am in community.

4. I feel in community when I am trusted with basic information about important issues relating to the shared mission. For example, instead of the silence that often surrounds budgetary cutbacks or realignments, I am told that decisions need to be made and why—and I am given adequate information about when, how, by whom, and on what basis they are being made. Nothing undercuts my sense of community more quickly than being kept in the dark about basic issues until "the day after."

5. I feel in community when I have a chance to voice my opinion on issues relating to the shared mission or my part of it—and I am given meaningful responses to what I have to say. I do not need to have my way all the time or even most of the time, but I need to know that my voice is wanted and heard.

In sum, I feel that I am in community when I feel seen, known, and respected—when I am taken seriously and appreciated, not just for the function I perform but for who I am as a person. Community is about power *and* rewards *and* relationships *and* meaning—and there will always be imbalances among us in those regards. But we can go a long way toward community by understanding that imbalances in one area can often be corrected, or at least relieved, by rebalancing in another.

There are many practical steps we can take to help community happen. This is not the place to spell them out in great detail, but here are three possibilities that can be realized either on small college campuses or within human-scale units of a large university:

• People often spend decades working alongside each other without knowing much, if anything, about who the others are, how they are, why they are here, or where they are going. The absolute minimum in building community is to learn at least a little bit about each other's stories. We could begin small staff or committee meetings with a simple autobiographical question that each person has a few minutes to answer aloud: "Tell us about an important older person in your life." "Tell us about the first dollar you ever made." "Tell us about the best vacation you ever took." Questions like these are nonthreatening and can be answered on any level of vulnerability a person chooses. But the cumulative effect of asking and answering them over a period of months and years is the growth of interpersonal understanding and a deepening sense of community.

• Though much of our work in institutions must be done through a division of labor, with different people pursuing different specializations, it is possible from time to time to find work that can be shared for the sake of community building. In a school where I once worked, there was an annual mass mailing to alumni and other constituents to solicit financial support. The mailing could have been done by a machine or by an outside "service provider." Instead, we gathered the entire staff once a year, for the better part of a day, and together we folded papers and stuffed envelopes, sang and laughed and told tales, and enjoyed each other's company.

• Every institution could profit from examining its own processes of information sharing and decision making through the lens of exclusion and inclusion. In many colleges and universities, for example, the proportion of adjunct faculty has increased dramatically over the past decade. But during that same decade, information sharing and decision making has proceeded apace, as if all the faculty were full-time, either tenured or on a tenure track. The good that would come from including adjunct faculty as trust holders of the institution cannot be overestimated—and its impact would be felt not only in improved morale but in teaching effectiveness as well.

Community in Teaching and Learning

Closely examined, the phrase "community in teaching and learning" is redundant; without community, there can be no teaching or learning worthy of the name. But it is a redundancy worth uttering because teaching and learning are so often reduced to a one-to-one exchange of information in which "community" is regarded as neither achievable nor desirable. Students are gathered in one place, called the classroom, not for the sake of community but merely to make it unnecessary for the professor to deliver the information more than once.

By now we have more than enough research (to say nothing of personal experience) to know that the fastest and deepest learning happens when there is a dynamic community of connections between teacher and student and subject. The student who feels related to a subject is motivated to do the hard work called learning. That relationship is often mediated by a professor to whom the student feels connected in the first place and strengthened by building relations with other students who are engaged in the process.

As I argue at length in my book *The Courage to Teach* (1998), the danger in insisting on making community a key component of teaching and learning is that people will try too quickly to translate community into a technique, for example, collaborative learning. But good teaching can never be reduced to technique. If you want to prove the point, simply collect a dozen student stories of good teachers they have had and notice how seldom technique is mentioned—and how, when it is mentioned, there is great variation among the techniques that good teachers use.

To say that community is key to teaching and learning and then translate that into small circles of students engaged in analyzing case studies or solving problems is to diminish the possibilities inherent in the idea and to marginalize faculty whose disciplines or personal gifts do not lend themselves to this approach.

We need a more capacious view of what community in teaching and learning might mean, which is why I have found myself talking less about *community*—a word that is so easily reified—and more about *a capacity for connectedness*. If we could ask ourselves critical questions about our own capacity for connectedness and our strategies for developing that capacity in our students, we might discover more and more ways to create community in the classroom without confining the concept to its most conventional forms.

As an acid test of my point, let me take the much-maligned pedagogy called lecturing, which is often criticized these days as tragically anticommunal, little more than the egocentric performance of a "sage on the stage," as contrasted with the community-building mentoring of a "guide by the side." That caricature began to fall apart for me as I thought back over my own education, which was graced, from time to time, by a lecturer who created a palpable and powerful sense of community in session after session after session.

How can a lecture course create community when, for fifty minutes, the classroom is dominated by one voice? The answer, of course, involves the motivations of the lecturer, what he or she is saying, and the ends he or she intends to serve. A lecture that emerges from "a capacity for connectedness" and evokes that same capacity in the listener has certain characteristics that distinguish it quite clearly from a lecture that cuts the connections off.

The latter is exemplified by the lecturer who tells you what the right questions are and gives you all the right answers, asking only your assent. But when a lecturer generates new questions right before your eyes, giving you a glimpse of where questions come from, then wrestles with those questions in open and vulnerable ways, a sense of connectedness is created among the listeners, who find themselves engaged in their own inner dialogue.

Similarly, when a lecturer simply rehearses "the facts of the matter" in a given field of study, expecting the listeners to commit them to memory, connectedness is shut down. But when a lecturer portrays the human drama from which those facts were generated—

when we learn not just the content of Marx's ideas but the personal and social dynamics that animated his mind—we are connected with the lecturer, the subject, and one another in surprising ways.

The communal consequences of a good lecture are much like those of good theater. When you attend a skillful production of a great drama, you are not a passive member of the audience. Far from it. You are deeply engaged in body, mind, and spirit with what is happening on stage. You need not be a member of the cast to be a participant in that community of meaning, for your own life is being evoked by the words of the playwright and the interpretations of the actors.

My insistence that a variety of teaching techniques have the potential to help create community should not be taken as a license to teach however one will. It should give us pause to note that the practice of lecturing is much more widespread in the academy than the practice of creating community through lecturing! There is a litmus test here, and it is a rigorous one. Does my pedagogy come from a place of connectedness in me so it can evoke in my students those connections that make learning possible? Or am I using my pedagogy in a way that distances me from my subject and sets me apart from my students, thus diminishing the chances that my classroom will become a place of live encounter?

If we could ask those questions openly and answer them honestly, we would take a meaningful step toward creating more community among teachers and students at the heart of academic life—without reducing community to one size that fails to fit all.

Community with the World

From its very inception, higher education has had an uneasy, even hostile, relation to the world around it; we tend to hold academic values in ways that set us apart. In fact, we sometimes hold our values as weapons against the world—a tendency driven deep into our institutional DNA.

Here is how the Columbia Accountability Study (1995) char-
acterizes the evolutionary starting point of the modern university:

> Since their medieval origins, universities have claimed
> special status, not as a privilege but as an essential pre-
> requisite to carrying out their mission. Universities arose
> from non-institutional gatherings of scholars. A great
> teacher would attract a following, often from faraway
> places. Soon the out-of-towners found themselves in
> need of protection, and so they banded together in guilds
> to obtain immunities from local interference, service
> obligations, and taxation [Graham, Lyman, and Trow,
> p. 5].

Do we still need protection today, so many centuries later? I do
not want to minimize the dangers of external assaults on academic
freedom (though I agree with the wag who said that academic freedom in recent decades has meant little more than the freedom to
be academic). But the protection we most need today is not from
the outside world but from ourselves: from our own tendencies toward arrogance and isolation, from our own self-protective and self-
defeating insularity, from our many ways of widening rather than
closing the gap between the academy and the world around us.

We can hold our values in ways that connect us creatively with
the world rather than set us apart. We can reach out for partnerships with others, and when we do, we may find that our values are
more widely shared than we imagine.

"The world" is a very large place, so I need to be selective in illustrating the kinds of partnerships I have in mind. I will offer just
one example as I bring this afterword to a close: the story of Princeton Project 55. It is a story that is not as well known as it deserves to
be and is instructive on at least two fronts: it gives us a model of creating community between the academy and world, and it tells us
something about transforming academic politics in order to get a
job done.

As they approached their fortieth reunion, the Class of 1955 at Princeton University decided to give their alma mater an unusual gift. Instead of a bell tower or a meditation garden or a major contribution to the endowment, they offered their influence and expertise in building a bridge between the university and the world—a bridge that would allow new generations of Princeton students to link their education with their emerging vocations and with a wide range of societal concerns.

The influence and expertise of the Class of '55 is considerable. Among their number are some who are quite visible in American public life, others who are not known publicly but who hold positions of real power, and still others whose lives have been quietly devoted to high purposes. Not every college could claim so many names in the first or second categories, perhaps, but every college has among its alumni countless people who know and serve the world well.

For several years prior to their fortieth reunion, members of the Class of '55 worked to generate both money for this project and, more important, administrative and faculty commitment to a partnership between the university and its alumni in the service of Princeton students. Using their connections, class members began to create internships and service-learning opportunities for undergraduates, and the faculty and administration began to explore the implications of such a program for finances, the academic calendar, course credit, curriculum, and pedagogy.

What ensued is impressive by any measure. In 1990, Princeton Project 55 launched its first initiative, with fourteen summer interns and eight year-long fellows being placed in significant positions with public interest organizations. Since that time, Project 55 has placed almost seven hundred students or recent graduates as interns and fellows in twenty cities around the country, while leveraging nearly $6 million in stipends and salaries for these students. The leaders of Project 55 estimate that these students, through their work with public interest organizations, have touched the lives of some five million Americans. (Supporting documents and additional information on Project 55 can be found on the Web at http://www. project55.org/Index.html.)

These data are impressive. But even more impressive to me is that, from the outset, the Class of '55 started using its authority in the life of the university to open a new dialogue about curriculum and pedagogy—about community at the heart of academic life.

In 1995, the group—which had by then expanded to include alumni from every decade since the fifties—issued a discussion paper titled "Princeton University in the 21st Century: Paths to More Effective Undergraduate Education." In the preface, the writers announce their intentions in words both substantive and bold, words of a sort not often uttered by alumni to their alma mater:

> This paper makes the case for a new approach to undergraduate education at Princeton, an approach that takes account of research that:
>
> • Increasingly illuminates how individuals learn most effectively;
>
> • Reflects a growing consensus on what students need to know to function more effectively as individuals, citizens, and workers; and
>
> • Suggests the curricular and pedagogical approaches most responsive to new knowledge and new needs.
>
> It is time for even the greatest of our institutions of higher education and research to think in different ways. As they do so, the first requirement will be for clarity about, and a shared definition of, basic institutional purposes. So that readers will understand our perspectives in what follows, we note our belief that Princeton's purposes should be:

- Nurturing (not merely "teaching") reflective, caring, able citizens;

- Discovering important knowledge and truths; and

- Serving society's civic, economic, and social needs.

Secondly, we intend this paper to be a strong argument for experiential education at Princeton. The contemporary definition of experiential education is:

Learning activities that engage the learner in the phenomenon being studied. It assumes (and we cannot stress this point too strongly) that the experience is closely linked to a course, is overseen by a teacher, and is subjected to active, collaborative reflection with peers and others in the classroom and elsewhere on campus.

Exploring all that we might learn from Princeton Project 55 is beyond the scope of this book. But the most important insight the story offers, it seems to me, is this: among all the constituencies of our academic institutions, alumni may be in the best position to help us create more community between the academy and the world and to do so in ways that respect core academic values. They are also the constituency least often called upon for purposes such as these—or for any purpose other than financial support!

Ever since I learned about Princeton Project 55, I have been pondering a critical question: Why do we who care about educational reform either ignore the alumni or wait for them to approach us, as the Class of 1955 approached Princeton? Why do we not reach out to the graduates of our institutions for assistance in building bridges between the academy and the world?

What alumni can bring to this bridge building is not only energy, knowledge, contacts, and financial resources. They also bring a new force to the politics of academic reform, which is much in need of new forces! In very short order, Project 55 broke through the historic resistance of many academic institutions, especially elite institutions, to anything that takes them out of their comfort zone. They were able to do so for at least three reasons: (1) the alumni are a legitimate constituency of the university; (2) their approach to the university was deeply respectful of its integrity and yet appropriately critical of its limitations; and (3) they represent real power in the university's life.

As we pursue our efforts to fulfill the promise of the academy by deepening the communal relations of administration, faculty, staff, and students, let us not forget the needs of the larger world—or our own need for the new perspectives and energies that exchange with that world can bring. Perhaps we have planted the seeds of our own transformation by educating generations of students who left the academy, became good citizens of that larger world, and can now turn around and help us become good citizens, too.

References

Graham, P. A., Lyman, R. W., and Trow, M. (1995). Accountability of colleges and universities: An Essay. In *The Accountability Study*. New York: Columbia University. Available at:
Http://Info.library.emory.edu/FryeInstitute/Readings/17141501.pdf
Palmer, P. J. (1998). *The courage to teach*. San Francisco: Jossey-Bass.

Index

A

About Messiah (brochure), 48, 50
Academic culture, 179. *See also* Collegiate community
Academic Duty (Kennedy), 4
ACPA (American College Personnel Association), 140
Agape Center for Service and Learning (Messiah College), 64–65
Agenda of common caring, 7
An Aristocracy of Everyone (Barber), 102
Asian Student Fellowship (Messiah College), 63
Astin, A. W., 137, 138, 147, 151
Astin, H. S., 138
The Astonishing Hypothesis: The Scientific Search for the Soul (Crick), 16

B

Bacon, J. L., 121, 126, 169
Barber, B., 102, 105
Barber, B. R., 138
Bellah, R. N., 1, 136, 146, 151
Biddle, M. E., 96, 100, 102, 113
Bolman, L., 16
Bonner Foundation, 110
Boorstin, D., 12
Boyer, E. L., 8, 10, 21, 49, 50, 52, 64, 67, 72, 73, 78, 93, 94, 95, 105, 107, 111, 137, 138, 146, 151, 166, 175

Boyer Fellows (Carson-Newman College), 108, 110–112, 172–173
Boyer, K., 111
Boyer Laboratory for Learning. *See* Carson-Newman Laboratory for Learning
Boyer model: assessing quality of student experience in, 31–32; Carson-Newman College adoption of, 93–95, 101–106; on forming just/caring ethos, 26–27; on influencing responsible behaviors, 27–28; Penn State's focus on, 21–22; on relating classroom learning to real life, 36–37; strategic themes of, 23
Boyer Principles: benefits to campus climate by, 42; Carson-Newman College use of, 93–95, 101–106; learning program using, 34t; Oregon State conversation model use of, 75, 78–80; overview of, 22–24; students on campus climate and, 40t
Boyer Scholars (Carson-Newman College), 173
Brazzell, J., 145, 167
Brensinger, T., 48
Brethren in Christ, 46, 47
Bringle, R. G., 140
Brown, C. E., 93, 97, 169

Brown, J. M., 93, 169
Bucher, G., 57, 62

C

Campus climate: assessing, 39–41; assessing differential impact on, 41–42; Boyer Principles benefits to, 42; creating "just community," 9, 26–27; specialization influence on SUNY, 140–141. *See also* Boyer model; Collegiate community
Campus Compact: A Statement of Vision, Values and Commitments (Oregon State), 76–77
Campus Compact (Oregon State). *See* Oregon State Campus Compact
Campus Compact (Penn State), 28
Campus Life: In Search of Community (Boyer), 1, 71, 107–108, 145
Campus Life, 16
Capacity for connectedness, 186
Caring community, 9
Carleton College, 180
Carnegie Classification Report, 151, 155–156t, 158
The Carnegie Foundation for the Advancement of Teaching, 10, 94, 166
Carson-Newman College: Christian mission of, 104–106; impact of Boyer's philosophy on, 93–95, 101–106; STL financial backing of, 93; "Victorian Christmas" celebration of, 15, 100, 112
Carson-Newman College community-building: application of Boyer's philosophy to equality of, 104–106; Boyer-inspired collaboration for, 93–95, 101–106; fostered through co-curricular experiences, 97–99; Laboratory for Learning to promote, 96–101; next step for, 172–173; progress and success of, 106–107; promoting integrated participation for, 101–104
Carson-Newman Laboratory for

Learning: administrative team profile of, 110–111; assessing impact of, 114–118; Boyer's endorsement and dedication of, 111–112; Christian mission promoted through, 104–106; co-curricular experiences of, 97–99; development of, 96–97; facilitating success of, 106–107; goals of, 99–101; next community-building step by, 172–173; organizational schematic of, 107–111, 109e; pragmatic application of, 112–114; Steering Team of, 108, 110; stimulating integrated participation, 101–104
Carson-Newman Residence Life Department, 99, 114
Carter, A. W., 21, 169
Celebrative community, 9–10
Change magazine, 16, 18
"Citizenship and Voting in an Election Year" (Penn State survey), 38
Civic education, 136–140
Climie, N., 118
College: The Undergraduate Experience (Boyer), 10
Collegiate community: complexity of motive/method of, 11–16; creating condition for creating, 174–178; CUCI definition of, 148, 159; examining the, 1–2; five markers for building, 182–183; identifying commitment to shared vision of, 170–171; institutional contributions to, 172; knowing, teaching, learning mission of, 179–180; nature of, 8–11; need to assess students' perceptions of, 145–147; obstacles to building efforts to, 171; relationship between the world and, 187–192; seven activities to build, 175–176; soul of the, 16–18; student-community development specialization approach to, 123–142; three practical options

for, 183–184; uniting force of curiosity and wonder in, 18–19. *See also* Campus climate

Columbia Accountability Study, 188

Common caring agenda, 7

Community: agenda of common caring/shared purpose and, 7; contributions of solitude to, 5–6; CUCI definition of, 148, 159; examining the meaning of, 2–7; formed by W.W. II prisoners, 5–6; importance of balance in, 3–4; "just," 9, 26–27

Community service, 136–140

"Community Volunteering and Service Learning" (Penn State survey), 38–39

Conversation model (Oregon State), 75–80

Cooper, G., 4

Council of Christian Colleges and Universities, 47

The Courage to Teach (Palmer), 185

Crick, F., 16, 17

CUCI (College and University Community Inventory): community as defined by, 148, 159; conclusions reached by, 157–158; findings of, 152–153t, 154–155; new student response measures of, 164–165; origins and purpose of, 147–148, 150–152; scores by Carnegie Classification, 151, 155–156t, 158; six categories of, 148, 149e–150e; suggested design modifications of, 159–164e; suggestions for expanding administration of, 165

Cureton, J. S., 146

D

Deal, T., 16

Democratic values education, 136–140

The Demon Haunted World (Sagan), 12

Dey, E., 147

Disciplined community, 9

The Discoverers (Boorstin), 12

The Disuniting of America (Schlesinger), 13

E

Ecclesiastes 4:9–11, 3

Elliott, J., 101

Enerson, D., 32, 39

Ernest L. Boyer Laboratory for Learning, 111. *See also* Carson-Newman Laboratory for Learning

Ethos education (Messiah College), 52

Etzioni, A., 1, 3–4

Eyler, J., 138

F

Faculty/staff: community in teaching and, 185–187; community-building experienced through, 180–182; community-building obstacles by, 171; identifying commitment to shared vision by, 170–171

Faculty/staff (Carson-Newman): Laboratory for Learning role by, 98–99; New Men's Hall sleep-out for, 105; programmatic compartmentalization of, 94; student survey on, 117–118

Faculty/staff (Messiah College): "Chat-n-Chew" program and, 58–59; Community of Educators role by, 52; Teaching Excellence Award for, 55; Welcome Week role by, 56

Faculty/staff (Penn State): using active "learning" experiences, 36–37; on-line resource for Penn State, 25–26; "Quality of Instruction" study assessing, 32–36; role in building "just community" by, 26–27; sense of community fostered by, 24

Fincher, C., 16

Fishing at Emmert's Cove (Marion), 113
Fountainhead, The (Rand), 4
Frankl, V., 6
Fresh Start, 29

G

Galileo, G., 12
Gamble, A., 102–103
Gardner, J., 8
Gibran, K., 5, 7
Giles, D. E., Jr., 138
Gilkey, L., 5
Glassick, C. E., 105
Goldstein, M., 135
Graham, C., 117–118
Griswold, C., 151

H

Habitat for Humanity, 29
Habits of the Heart (Bellah and others), 1
Hall, C., 100, 113
Hatcher, J. A., 140
Hateful acts (addressed by Penn State), 26–27
Huber, M. T., 105

I

Individualism, 4–5
Integrative community development model of specialization, 135–136

J

Janota, J., 32, 39
"Journey to a Hate-Free Millennium" (video), 27
"Just community" concept: basis of, 61–62; creating campus climate using, 9, 26–27

K

Kennedy, D., 4
King, M. L., Jr., 12
Koinonia Week (Messiah College), 65–66
Kuh, G., 1, 95

L

La Alianzia Latina (Messiah College), 63
Laboratory for Learning: Promoting Community Learning Across Curricular and Co-curricular Functions (Biddle, Lee, and McDonald), 96
"Late Night Penn State" activity, 37
Leadership: campus compact and, 72; community service to develop, 28–29; Oregon State conversation model to construct, 74–78; SUNY School of Social Welfare opportunities for, 136–140
Leading with Soul (Bolman and Deal), 16
Learning: assessing outcomes of, 36–37; assessing purposeful, 32–36; community in, 185–187; components of quality educational environment for, 33t; creating ethos of, 53–54; fit with Boyer Principles, 34t; Messiah College common, 56–57; service, 139–140
Lee, E. D., 96, 100, 102
Lee University, 15
Levine, A., 146
Levine, J. H., 146
Littleton, R. A., 93, 97, 169
Longerbeam, S. D., 69

M

Mabry, J. B., 138
McDonald, W. M., 93–94, 96, 97, 100, 102, 106, 107, 113, 114, 126, 131, 142, 145, 148, 169
Maeroff, G. I., 105
Man's Search for Meaning (Frankl), 6
Marion, J. D., 113
Marotta, S., 138
Marsden, G., 16, 17
Marx, K., 187
Memphis Symphony Orchestra, 2–3
Messiah College: core purpose/focus of, 45–46; description of, 46–49; history of shared identity by, 45;

lessons offered by, 66–67; provost model for education used by, 52

Messiah College "Chat-n-Chew" program, 58–59

Messiah College "Community Covenant," 52–54

Messiah College Community of Educators, 52

Messiah College community-building: administrative organization/governance for, 51–52; Agape Center for, 64–65; using celebration for, 65; clarifying institutional identity for, 49; common learning and, 56–57; "Community Covenant" and, 52–54; educator development and, 58–59; using ethos education, 52; foundational values for, 51; identity statement/mission statement for, 49–50; Koinonia Week and, 65–66; Micah Partnership and, 61–63; Multicultural Council and, 63–64; next step in, 173; partnership and, 59; Provost Seminar used for, 57–58; reflections and application of, 66–67; residence-based academic learning and, 59–60; "significance of community" value and, 48; Welcome Week and, 54–56; Wittenburg Door and, 60–61

Messiah College Family Weekend, 57

Messiah College Multicultural Council, 63–64

Messiah College "People, Ideas and Machines: A Twentieth-Century Retrospective," 56–57

Messiah College "Scholarship Colloquies" sessions, 59

Messiah College Service Day, 64–65

Messiah College Tapestry Week, 64

Messiah College "The Christian Imagination" program, 60

Micah Partnership (Messiah College), 61–63

Miller, J., 1

Minority students: impact on campus climate by, 41–42; Penn State on hateful acts against, 26–27

Mitchell, B., 12

Moore, B. L., 21, 32, 39, 169

Moore, T., 16

Moses, D., 180–181

Moses, R., 180–181

Multicultural education (Messiah College), 61–63

N

Nashman, H., 138

NASPA (National Association of Student Personnel Administrators), 140

NASPA's Innovative Programs Award, 111

National Center for Service Learning, 28

Neal, P., 4

New York Times, 27, 36

New York University LGBT Student Center, 131

Newman, F., 16, 18

Newspaper Readership Program (Penn State), 21

No Future Without Forgiveness (Tutu), 7

O

Oberst, G., 138

100 Classic Books About Higher Education (Fincher and others), 16

Open community, 9

Oregon State Campus Compact: assumptions included in, 76–78; definitions created for, 79; initiatives designed for, 80–82; lessons of, 88–90; Rights and Responsibilities initiative of, 84–87; what didn't work in, 87–88

Oregon State Division of Student Affairs: Boyer's Principles and conversation model used by, 78–80; Campus Compact adopted by, 84; challenges of, 69–71; conversation model to construct leadership agenda of, 74–78; leadership model adopted by, 71–74

Oregon State University: challenges of, 69–71; demographics of, 69; next community-building step by, 173

P

Palmer, P. J., 49, 95, 96, 146, 147, 169, 179

Penn State AT&T Center for Service Leadership, 26

Penn State "Campus Climate for LGBT Students Survey," 40–41

Penn State College of Education, 26

Penn State Community Education Services, 26

Penn State community-building: academic alliances used to fashion, 24; assessing outcomes of, 31–32; Boyer model used for, 21–22; using campus dialogues for, 26–27; developing leadership through, 28–29; to influence responsible behaviors, 27–28; next step in, 174; role of technology in, 25–26; strategic planning for, 22–24; student service goals for, 29–31

Penn State Counseling and Psychological Services, 26

Penn State "Diversity Climate Survey," 40

Penn State Residence Hall Newspaper Readership Program, 36–37

Penn State Residence Life, 26, 30–31, 35–36

Penn State "Satisfaction Survey for Spring 2002," 40–41

Penn State Student Health Services, 26

Penn State's Office of Student Affairs Research and Assessment, 35

Penn State's Student Affairs Curriculum, 22–24

Pennsylvania State University: assessing campus climate of, 39–41; diversity of student population of, 21; student drinking addressed by, 37–38

Peterson, M., 151

Pew Charitable Trust, 93, 107

Phi Omega Chi (People of Color United for Christ) [Messiah College], 63

Postman, N., 13, 14

Preston, F., 135

Princeton Project 55, 188–192

"Princeton University in the 21st Century: Paths to More Effective Undergraduate Education" (Princeton Project 55), 190

Provost Seminar (Messiah College), 57–58

Purposeful community, 8–9

Q

"Quality of Instruction" study, 32–36, 33t

R

"Race in America" (*New York Times*), 27

Rand, A., 4–5

Remembering the Heart of Higher Education (Palmer), 95

Residence Life (Penn State), 26, 30–31, 35–36

"Residence Life Satisfaction Survey" (Carson-Newman College), 114–115

"Residence and Student Learning" survey (Penn State), 35–36

"Residential Teams" concept, 99. *See also* Carson-Newman Laboratory for Learning

"Resource Guide for Faculty" (Penn State on-line resource), 25–26

"Retaining the Legacy of Messiah College" (Boyer address), 50

Roark, H. (*The Fountainhead* character), 4, 5

Roper, L. D., 69, 169

S

Sagan, C., 12

"Saving Higher Education's Soul" (Newman), 16, 18

Sawatsky, R. J., 49, 50

Schlesinger, A., 13

Segall, J., 135

Semmelweiss, I., 12

Service learning, 139–140

Shantung Compound (Gilkey), 5, 6

Shapiro, N. S., 146

Shared purpose vision, 7

Sider, E. M., 45

"Significance of community" value, 48

Social change model, 138

Solitude, 5–6

Solitude (Storr), 5

The Soul of the American University (Marsden), 16, 17

Soul Mates (Moore), 16

Southern Adventist University, 15

The Spirit of Community (Etzioni), 1, 3–4

Staff. *See* Faculty/staff

Statement of Principle (Penn State), 21

Stein, J., 135

Storr, A., 5

"Strengthening Teaching and Learning in the First Two Years (STL)" [Pew Charitable Trust], 93

Student drinking, 37–38

"Student Experience and Satisfaction" study, 36

Student-community development specialization (SUNY): components of, 125–126; curriculum of, 126–130; field practicum of, 130–131; future goals of, 141–142; integrative community development model of, 135–136; international component of, 132–133; leadership symposium on, 131–132; SUNY School of Social Welfare use of, 123–125

Students: community-building obstacles by, 171; CUCI conclusions regarding, 157–158; CUCI created to assess community needs of, 147–152; CUCI findings on, 152–153t, 154–155; identifying commitment to shared vision by, 170–171; need to assess campus community perceptions of, 145–147

Students (Carson-Newman College): assessing impact of Boyer lab on, 114–118; Boyer Principles used to enhance, 95; co-curricular experiences of, 97–99; New Men's Hall sleep-out for, 105

Students (Messiah College): creating ethos of learning for, 53–54; honored as Boyer Scholars, 55; "The Christian Imagination" program and, 60

Students (Oregon State): initiatives for transition needs of, 80–82; programs established for, 82–84; Rights and Responsibilities initiative for, 84–87

Students (Penn State): assessing personal values of, 37–39; Boyer model and quality of experience by, 31–32; on Boyer Principles and their campus climate, 40t; "Quality of Instruction" study assessing, 32–36; Residence Hall Newspaper Readership Program for, 36–37

Students (SUNY): community service/leadership opportunities for, 136–140; student-community development specialization program and, 125–136

SUNY Americorps Fellows, 134–135

SUNY Annual Student-Community Wellness Leadership Symposium, 140

SUNY Reginald C. Wells Commuter Student Services Fellowship, 133–134

SUNY Reginald C. Wells Multicultural Affairs Fellowship, 133–134

SUNY School of Social Welfare: description of, 122; fellowships of, 133–135; future specialization goals of, 141–142; graduate assistantships of, 133; integrative community development model used by, 135–136; international component of specialization at, 132–133; leadership opportunities through, 136–140; leadership symposium sponsored by, 131–132; specialization curriculum developed by, 126–130; specialization field practicum by, 130–131; student-community development specialization by, 123–126

SUNY (State University of New York) at Stony Brook: fellowships at, 133–135; graduate assistantships at, 133; introduction to, 122; next community-building step by, 174; specialization impact on campus community of, 140–141

"Symphony No. 1 in C Minor" (Brahms), 2

T

Teaching/community link, 185–187. *See also* Faculty/staff

Technology, community building role of, 25–26

Templeton Foundation, 112

Tompkins, J., 1

Tutu, Bishop D., 7

2000 presidential election, 12

U

USA Today, 36

W

Watson, J., 17

Wells, C. A., 45, 169

Willits, F., 32, 39

Wittenburg Door (Messiah College), 60–61

Wood, G., 118

Z

Zemsky, R., 146, 169